Intertwined

Our Happiness Is Tied to God's Glory

By Mark Ballenger

Copyright © 2017 by Mark Ballenger

ISBN-13:
978-1548333362

ISBN-10:
1548333360

For blogs, free eBooks, and more resources by Mark Ballenger, please visit ApplyGodsWord.com.

Contact us at:
Twitter: @Apply_GodsWord
Facebook: www.facebook.com/ApplyGodsWord/
Website: ApplyGodsWord.com
Email: markballenger@applygodsword.com

They will be my people, and I will be their God. And I will give them one heart and one purpose: to worship me forever, for their own good and for the good of all their descendants. And I will make an everlasting covenant with them: I will never stop doing good for them. I will put a desire in their hearts to worship me, and they will never leave me. I will find joy doing good for them and will faithfully and wholeheartedly replant them in this land.

-Jeremiah 32:38-41(NLT)

Table of Contents

Introduction

I believe there is a growing longing in the church today. It's a longing for a deeper, fuller explanation of the reality in which we find ourselves. We know that God loves us. We know that he came to save us. But somehow we also know this is not the full story.

When I recommitted my life to the Lord as a teenager, my heart was aching for a deep, rich encounter with God. I knew he had saved me from a life of rebellion; but as I searched for him, I continued to run into the fluff. The "fluff" is that feeling you get when someone seeks to make their view of God so amazing, you feel it somehow diminishes the real thing with every well meant, flowery description they give. Buried inside our hearts is the hope that there is more to Christianity than most of us have been given.

I believe there is. Without diminishing the truth that God has an overwhelmingly strong desire to see us prosper, I must admit I find God teaching me there is more to the story than my current earthly prosperity. To cut to the chase, I believe the rich, fulfilling story we all long to be a part of centers around one little phrase: God's glory.

These two words may seem slightly anticlimactic to some Christians since they have probably heard both of them about fifty-times last Sunday alone, "Glory to God, Bob," "Amen, Carl! Give him all the glory this morning."

But words are worthless if we don't know what they mean. My hope is that this book will help us understand the massive importance in understanding these two little words. I am convinced once we have a deeper understanding of God's desire for his own magnification in this broken world and we join him in this pursuit, our desire for a richer story to live in will be satisfied in the process even when our external lives seem rather unimpressive.

So what is God's glory anyway? I think we have heard this phrase so much it has become part of the fluff we all subconsciously cringe over when it meets our ears. But we must not become numb to God's glory, for it is the very purpose for which we were made. In Isaiah 43:6-7, when God is calling his sons and daughters, he refers to them as those "whom I created for my glory, whom I formed and made." Therefore, if we lose focus of God's glory, we will lose focus on the meaning of our life.

"The glory of God," "glorify God," and words like "glorification" are used in a variety of ways throughout the Bible, so to give one definition is difficult. However, without going into a deep hermeneutical dialogue about these words, in general an overarching biblical definition for "the glory of God" is when the invisible qualities of God are made visible or knowable. For example:

- When Moses asked to see the glory of God, the Lord said, "I will make all my goodness pass before you and will proclaim before you my name 'The LORD' (Exodus 33:19). The Lord showed Moses his glory by making his goodness visible and knowable to Moses.

- In Isaiah 6:3 it states, "Holy, holy, holy is the LORD of hosts; the whole earth is full of his glory!" You'd think it would say, "the whole earth is full of his holiness." But when the holiness of God is on display throughout the earth, it's called glory.

- Men and women were made for the glory of God (Isaiah 43:7), therefore men and women are made in the image of God (Genesis 1:27). When we bear his image properly, we display his character and thus glorify him. When we disobey him and thus do not reflect him well, we sin and "fall short of the glory of God" (Romans 3:23).

- As God himself, Jesus Christ glorifies God the best because he visibly reveals God the most and makes God known more than anyone or anything else (John 1:18, Colossians 1:15, Hebrews 1:1-3).

God's glory is what he publicly displays about himself to show the world his greatness. When he makes his invisible character, qualities, and attributes visible and knowable, this is what we mean by "God's glory."

We were made for one purpose and one purpose only: to display, reflect, worship, obey, lift up, or please God. There are so many words we could use to describe this singular purpose, but they all culminate in the verb "glorify." We were created to glorify God. That alone is our purpose.

Until we realize God did not make this world with us at the center of it, but rather with himself as central, the deepest longings of our hearts will continue to go unquenched. For when we dig to find what is at the root of our souls discontentment, we will discover the secret God continues to reveal to generation after generation of those saints looking for the cure to their dissatisfaction. When God's desire to show the world his beauty becomes our desire, the deep well of satisfaction we hoped existed is finally uncovered.

It seems contradictory at first, but when we lose ourselves in the purposes of God, only then are we truly found. For God's glorification and our good are not two different pursuits; by his beautiful design they are actually one. When we seek to praise God, we will discover we are actually seeking our own pleasure in the process. And when we find pleasure in God, we are praising God more powerfully than ever.

I didn't write this book to bash the church. There are enough books on the market with that intent. But I would be lying if I said I did not want to challenge her. I think there are trends right now in many of our own Christian communities that if we were all being honest about, we would admit don't sit well with us. Therefore, I hope this book is a call back to the reason why we all became followers of Christ to begin with, which was to love him who first loved us.

Knowing some of the things I am going to say may be a little jarring at times, my hope is that the influence of C.S. Lewis may bring some peace to my readers. I know in most Christian circles Lewis is rather trendy, and by nature I have always been slightly culturally rebellious, but at the risk of joining the Christian masses, I too must pay him homage. I wasn't aware of the intensity of his influence on me until I realized he had found his way into nearly every chapter of this book. So, honestly, rather than to deliberately find more varied sources to limit his voice, I embraced his regular appearance, and at times even sought it out so it was not absent for too long.

I don't believe Lewis is infallible, only more respected and wise than me. I think the truth can be rattling at times, so hopefully with Lewis walking beside us, saying similar things as I will be saying, we can be slightly more at ease with the discomfort truth often brings before it turns into peace. Obviously, however, this comfort should come mostly from the many Scripture verses quoted I believe form the bases of what I hope God's Spirit reveals to us in the coming pages.

Lastly, I'd like to mention the importance of John Piper on this book. You won't find many quotes from him in these pages. But when I was in my early twenties, I read a book by him that God used to transform my worldview, my theology, and more importantly the way I lived my life. The book was called *Desiring God* and in it Piper unpacks this premise, "God is most glorified in us when we are most satisfied in him."

This idea is rooted in Scripture. Piper calls this biblical principle "Christian Hedonism" and the idea captured in this phrase is that Christians should seek as much pleasure in God as possible because the way we glorify God is by finding joy in him. Therefore to obey the command to glorify the Lord, we must seek not only our salvation through Christ, but we must also find our satisfaction in Christ.

Without Piper's premise that God is most glorified in us when we are most satisfied in him, this book you are reading couldn't exist. That truth is the foundation of what is written here. *Intertwined* basically takes the next theological and practical step and says: Not only is God most glorified in us when we are most satisfied in him, but we are also most satisfied in him when God is most glorified in us.

In *Desiring God*, Piper has made the case that to glorify God we must find joy in him. In *Intertwined*, my goal was to make the case that to find joy in God we must seek to glorify him. God's glory and our good are intimately connected. Where his honor and our happiness begin and end is impossible to know because God has designed all this to wrap together. Our pleasure and God's praise are beautifully knitted into one another. Hence the title, *"Intertwined: Our Happiness Is Tied to God's Glory."*

Well friends, as we begin this journey together, I think it only proper for us to join in prayer to ask God for his blessing over us:

> Heavenly Father,
>
> Without you speaking through this book it will be totally worthless. We ask that we would not hear the words of a man but that every time we pick up this book, we would hear your Spirit speaking through it. Our desire is to please you. We ask that you would enhance our knowledge of you that our intimacy with you might grow as well. We ask for your grace, because it's all by grace, to experience your goodness. Thank you for who you are. We request that you would glorify yourself by showing us more of you. We love and thank you for loving us. In Jesus name, alone, we do pray. Amen."

1

Why Some and Not Others?

All that we call human history – money, poverty, ambition, war, prostitution, classes, empires, slavery – is the long terrible story of man trying to find something other than God which will make him happy. -C.S. Lewis[1]

Bring all who claim me as their God, for I have made them for my glory. It was I who created them. -Isaiah 43:7 (NLT)

How did it come to this? My face was like a stone but I was panicking internally. My chest was thumping like a deep drum. My head was spinning, clouded with too many thoughts to speak in coherent words and sentences. As I continued to push my daughter down the sidewalk in her stroller, a brisk gust of misty spring air chilled our cheeks.

Just then I saw him walking towards me from the other end of the street. I had to do a double-take to really make sure it was him, "Pastor Joe? Is that really you?"

"Mark!" he said lightheartedly. But after we locked eyes, he could tell all was not well.

What were the odds? I had gone on a walk with my daughter to clear my head and pray about doing one of the hardest things I've ever been asked to do. Our church was at a turning point. As the associate pastor, some of the elders asked me to confront certain issues head on during a meeting planned in two days from when I went on that walk and saw Pastor Joe. It was a meeting called specifically to confirm or negate our suspicions of things we could not support. Everyone knew it was going to be a tense meeting, but no one knew what the end result was going to be.

To make a long story short and to be respectful regarding the details of those involved, it didn't go well. Poof. Just like that, eight years of my ministry life was gone. I had spent four years serving as a member plus four more years serving on staff, and then it all simply vanished. After the meeting, the staff, including myself, felt individually compelled to resign. No one forced us. We all just felt led by the Lord that it was the morally right thing to do considering the circumstances. And none of us had jobs lined up.

I had a wife, two young children, a mortgage, and a broken heart. When I first went to seminary and imagined being a pastor, I never thought it would turn out like this.

So when I ran into Pastor Joe on my walk that day, I knew God was intertwining our paths again by no coincidence. You see, in the days just before I saw Pastor Joe I had literally contemplated calling him. I hadn't talked to him in a few years, but he was my old family pastor, so whenever I did not know what to do or where to turn, I usually ended up calling him. It was not the quantity of time we spent together through my past but rather the quality that's had such an impact on me. When someone's there for you during your most vulnerable times of need, that person earns a special place in your heart.

Over 25 years ago, Pastor Joe was a firsthand witness when my parents, members of his young church, went through their divorce. My dad and stepmom (when she wasn't my stepmom yet) were unfaithful towards my mom. But that was far from the end of the story, and Pastor Joe was there for it all. He saw how God had a plan for my family, a plan that included growing my mom and redeeming both my dad and stepmom. After witnessing many years of God working in these three, Pastor Joe even had my mom and stepmom give their testimony of forgiveness together at his church.

When I entered the ministry myself, Pastor Joe came one night to see me preach. I didn't know he was coming, but God had arranged a fitting sermon for the night of his visit. I was preaching from Psalm 51, the psalm David wrote out of repentance once he was finally convicted over his adultery with Bathsheba. It was a message about redemption, and Pastor Joe has had a first row seat for a lot of redemption in my family's life and in my own.

As a young man when I was finally coming back to God and did not know how to escape the addictive sins I found myself trapped under, Pastor Joe made time to help as he took me to breakfast. In my twenties when I needed counsel on how to godly progress from dating to marrying my future wife, he cleared his schedule to talk with me even though I had been attending a different church for years.

So when I ran into him on my walk that day, it was a huge reminder to me of the shear faithfulness of God towards me and my family through the many tough years of our past. Sure I was sad that I was losing so much with this ministry coming to an end. Losing the chance to pastor the people who had become my first real church family was deeply frustrating. But seeing Pastor Joe was like God saying to me, "Don't worry,

Mark. We've been here before. I'm going to walk you through this one too. If you stick with me through this storm, I'll bring good out of this just like I always do. It's going to be painful. It's not going to look like you think it should. But don't you remember how faithful I've been through the years? Don't you remember what I've taught you?"

As I hope to share with you through the pages ahead, there have been so many ups and downs for me in life. When I was three my parents divorced, when I was ten my dad had a massive stroke that altered all of our lives in significant ways, and through my ministry years as an adult there's been some big highs and devastating lows. Don't get me wrong, my life is not interesting enough to keep you turning the page. This is not meant to be a memoir. But through each chapter in my life, I feel like God has been removing another layer to the mystery of happiness.

How on earth are we supposed to find joy when life keeps turning out in ways we don't like? After the staff resigned and people started learning about all that happened at our church (it was a popular church that seemed so healthy), the different reactions people had were astonishing. Some people felt betrayed and left church completely. Others stayed and grew bitter at the masses of people who left. Others used this opportunity to push deeper into their walk with the Lord. They found new churches and they seem better off than ever. Why do some react so well during difficulties and some so poorly?

Many years ago, I remember a counseling session I had with Pastor Joe. Just before I got up to leave, he looked at me intensely and asked a question that's haunted me ever since,

"How did you turn out to follow Jesus? I see kids in my church who grow up in healthy families, with two faithful parents, who attend church their whole life, only to turn away from God later. Why do you think you've continued to seek Jesus and have not turned away?" That question popped into my mind again after seeing him on the street that day, pondering how I should respond to God as this beautiful ministry went up in flames.

I honestly can't remember how I answered the question as a young man the first time it was posed to me. I have some basic answers now: the power of God to aid us in perseverance, my mom's faithful prayers, my dad and stepmom's example of repentance, the work of the Holy Spirit, and most importantly the grace of Jesus Christ – surely endurance and joy always come from God's grace.

But this question continues to haunt me. Why some and not others? Why do some people turn from God when they have a rough childhood? Why do some people run from God when a church, ministry, or relationship they loved is ruined? Are my simple answers the only explanation for why some turn from God after sin and hardships while others press in deeper to know him more?

I believe God's grace is always the reason for anything good in our lives. But I would be lying if I said I didn't think there was a deeper explanation as well; not more true, but perhaps a fuller explanation of the truth. Again, I want to reiterate that the cure to life's problems always rest on the gospel of Jesus Christ alone. But when God's grace truly settles on someone, something happens to them which causes inner joy despite external problems.

What I feel God has shown me through all the different chapters of life – and more importantly, through each chapter I read in the Bible – is that our happiness was never meant to be tied to the circumstances of our life. There's some other source to our joy that God wants us to drink from. But what is it?

How can you lose your job, lose your health, lose your church, lose a loved one, lose your friends, lose your marriage, or lose all that you hold dear in this world, and then be expected to go on living with joy? And yet there are countless saints through the ages who have loved God more after going through these types of trials, not less. There are some, it seems, who have taken the Holy Spirit literally when he directed Paul to write, "Rejoice in the Lord always!" (Philippians 4:4).

So here's what I've learned. Here's what I hope for us to discover together in the pages ahead. What I have noticed about those who find joy in the Lord when others do not is that those with joy have had their hearts changed to focus on one thing – God's glory.

The Cure, Not the Cookie Cutter

Could every sin, every problem, every source of pain really be traced back to one thing? Imagine if there was a discovery in the medical community that proved every sickness, mental disorder, disease, or physical discomfort could be linked to one common problem, thus solved by one common solution. Cancer, diabetes, back pain, strokes, depression, skinned knees, headaches, bipolar disorders, colds, and food poisoning can now be instantly eradicated because of this one new drug. This would change everything.

In the very same way, there actually is this cure in the spiritual realm. Now before you write me off, hear me out. This is not a clever way of pitching you the watered down gospel message you've probably heard so many times, "Pray this pray and everything will be all good."

The remedy for our broken souls truly is Jesus alone (John 14:6), but I will not leave you with the five letters making up his name as the neat, cookie-cutter answer for every need. I would never deny the amazing truth that once we receive the grace of Jesus and repent we are no longer alienated from God. However, everyone who has begun to follow Christ knows from personal experience that life's problems were not instantly solved when the Holy Spirit entered their hearts.

Jesus made it impossible for us to claim Christianity will take away all our external troubles when he stated, "In this world you will have trouble. But take heart! I have overcome the world." He said take heart, don't fear, trust him (John 16:33, John 14:27, John 14:1). He didn't say life will now be easy because we know him. The Christian life is simple, but it is never easy. As soon as Jesus raised Lazarus from the dead the Pharisees started planning not only Jesus assassination but Lazarus' too (John 12:10). Likewise, if our conversions were genuine, our lives probably got much more complicated as well.

If we desire to have this cure to life's discontentment we must take the next step after conversion. When we come to Christ, it's like stepping onto a new trail in the woods. We will never experience all the beauties and scenic views ahead if we stop moving forward simply because we have found ourselves on the best trail. The next step on the Christian journey is to not only realize what Christ did but why he did it. Jesus didn't come to earth to fix all the things that annoy us. Although Jesus came to serve, he is not our maid. The popular teaching that Jesus is our helper reduces the Sovereign King of angel armies to a bus boy in need of a few tips for helping us out a bit.

He did come to serve, but we were not the main point and we never will be. Jesus came, ultimately, for one purpose and one purpose only – to glorify God. But in his singular desire to please his Father, we were also the singular focus of his saving mission on earth. For the trail to glorifying God and saving humans were not two separate paths for Christ, but one beautifully interwoven trail leading to the same destination.

Understanding this is like taking the first step forward on the path to receiving this cure for inner joylessness.

What Is This Really All About?

This book, I hope, is more than a quick fix. It's more than another step by step plan for us to live our best life now. It's not about creating a new philosophy or fad. This is about what God is about. This is about God's glory. For his glory is the key to explaining why everything exists. As Jonathan Edwards put it, "It appears that all that is ever spoken of in the Scripture as an ultimate end of God's works is included in that one phrase, 'the glory of God.'"[2] His glory is the Rosetta Stone for interpreting the language of real life with all its ups and downs. It explains the motivation behind every act of God.

I am promising you nothing in regards to your external circumstances. This life will always present difficulties in the physical realm because this world is broken through and through. However, when we have a right perspective of God's passionate love relationship with himself (and with us) and we join him in this, our hearts deepest discontentment will be solved and our greatest joy will be experienced regardless of our external circumstances.

To be entirely honest, this book is not so much about solving our problems. It's about discovering you and I and our problems are not the point at all. God's glorification is. And what is even more beautiful, to the praise of God's glorious grace, is that when we begin to live the purpose for which God made us, our internal problems are solved and we do experience our best life now. You see, God is so amazing and worthy of worship, not only does he put himself first, he glorifies himself through doing good for us; and when we glorify him, we experience our best possible life.

God's glory and our good are intimately intertwined for all of eternity.

Get this and you get everything. God's glorification is not a part of Christianity. It is Christianity's heartbeat. The glory of God is right at the center of everything. If the Christianity we have does not filter everything through the lens of God's plan to exalt himself, it is not as full and satisfying as it could be. God's love, God's holiness, God's grace, God's wrath, and all things pertaining to God are simply misrepresented if they are not seen through the lens of his mission to show his divine beauty to the entire universe.

Along with this, if we do not see our personal lives (our jobs, vacations, dinner time, marriages, parenting, friendships, est.) through the lens of God's plan to magnify himself in front of a watching world, life will be full of turning good things into idols that can never fill our heart's deep longings put there by God. These are bold words, and I don't write them for boldness sake or to offend. I write them because I believe they are true, and only the truth can set us free (John 8:32).

I am not the point. You are not the point. Even Jesus saving us was not the ultimate point. From start to finish the workings of God center around one person . . . God.

Discontentment Disappears When Pleasing God Becomes Your Highest Aim

It sounds odd to say, but if we are truly being honest, there's really no other way to say it: God is for God first and foremost. This, however, is not the only point God seeks to make clear in his word. God is for God first and foremost, a point we will explore together, but God being for himself is also the best thing for us. The Bible makes it abundantly clear: We are not the point but we definitely are the benefactors.

So the three intertwined truths I hope to expose are:

1. God is most concerned with his own glory.

2. God desires the best for us, which is for us to glorify him.

3. God brings himself glory through doing us good.

We must understand all of these points because if we separate them from each other, we no longer have the truth and our miseries will quickly abound. If we deny that God blesses us immensely, we no longer have the God of the Bible but a selfish, unloving God. If we separate God's motive to magnify himself from his blessings given to us, God is no longer the center of all things, we are.

The church is like a beautiful skyscraper. We can make it look pretty on the outside and even be really busy on the inside, but if the foundation is off the whole thing is coming down. God's plan for complete worship of himself is the foundation of everything that exists. Remove it and a great crash is sure to follow.

Many of our problems are caused because we have swallowed Satan's lie and come to believe God is more like Santa Clause than he is the loving and holy God pictured in the Bible. We have magnified the things we see God doing for us and totally forgotten the reasons why he does them, and this has caused much instability to our Christian foundation. We have isolated the love of God for us and passively separated it from the total picture God seeks to reveal about himself.

So to answer the question posed at the beginning of this chapter: Why do some have joy while others do not? To put it simply, all of our discontentment in life will disappear by glorifying God because every problem occurs when we place ourselves above his glory.

When I view God, the universe, and everything in between as though it all revolves around making me happy, I become angry at everyone for failing the mission. However, when I view all of life through the lens of God's plan for praise, all of life is simplified because I can relax in knowing everything revolves around God's will, not mine. Like soldiers so committed to winning the war their immense joy is to serve in the most dangerous of places for the greater good, so too the Christian finds their joy when their sole desire is to please God at whatever cost to themselves.

When we live as though our life is no longer our own, only then do we begin to really live. Paul was content with little or much because he learned to equate his strength with Christ's strength, his happiness with Christ's happiness, his good with God's glory. He had learned if Christ was exalted, no matter the personal circumstance it brought him, he would be totally satisfied:

> . . . for I have learned to be content
> whatever the circumstances. I know what it is to

> be in need, and I know what it is to have plenty.
> I have learned the secret of being content in any
> and every situation, whether well fed or hungry,
> whether living in plenty or in want. I can do all
> this through him who gives me strength.
> (Philippians 4:11-13)

> And I trust that my life will bring honor to
> Christ, whether I live or die. (Philippians 1:20
> NLT)

God's motive in everything is to display his worthiness of
worship and when our purpose is intertwined with his, he
rewards us with our best possible life. God made it this way,
and until we live as though we truly believe God is center, our
lives will be wasted and we will feel the pain of our failure.
The cure to all of life's problems is simple, not easy, but
simple: Discontentment disappears when our sole desire is to
please him in every situation of life, through pain and pleasure.

My friends, God's glorification in our personal lives is the key
to everything for which our hearts were made. And so the rest
of this book is dedicated to realigning our understanding of
reality in light of this truth. The truth expressed in the full
gospel of Christ crucified and raised from the dead for the
glory of God is our path to deep intimacy with God and
unimaginable freedom (John 8:32). The truth is all that matters.

2

His Supremacy and Our Satisfaction

The great difficulty is to get modern audiences to realize that you are preaching Christianity solely and simply because you happen to think it true; they always suppose you are preaching it because you like it or think it good for society or something of that sort. -C.S. Lewis[1]

I want you to know that I am not doing this for your sake, declares the Sovereign Lord. -Ezekiel 36:32

(Note: The names and minor details of this story have been changed to protect people's identities.)

Jose was a drug addict. Although much older now and obviously a different man, his rough, tattooed exterior and muscular build allowed for an easy visual of his former life of crime. By his own admission, he had lived a crazy existence full of violence, quick pleasures, and self-centeredness. Eventually his rebellious ways brought him to jail. It was there God found him. The prison chaplain led Jose to accept Christ and he never looked back. He even went to seminary and began a career in counseling other men who had fallen into the same traps he had.

It was years later when I met Jose. He was sharing his testimony with a group of juvenile delinquents at the prison where our church was serving. The first part of Jose's testimony was quite common. God saved him, God delivered him, God helped him. The tears in his eyes were very telling to those of us who listened. God obviously did a lot for this man and he was clearly very appreciative.

But then Jose stopped. He told everyone what he had shared up to this point wasn't his full testimony. He wanted to play a DVD to explain the rest. The video rolled. It was a recording of a news program. A loud and stereotypical "breaking news" intro played. As the story unfolded, the reporter explained a young man on drugs had been running around a local neighborhood naked, breaking house windows, and threatening people with a knife.

A clip from the police car's dash-cam showed a blurry video of the nude young man running over the windshield. He looked wild and tortured, as if he was totally out of his mind. The reporter went on to explain the young man had come at police officers with the knife, forcing them to shoot and kill him.

It was here where the news story switched to an interview of the young man's parents. The mother was explaining she didn't blame the police officers for shooting her son but hoped God would somehow use this horrible tragedy to help others. Then came a clip of the father.

It was Jose. As he stood there in the middle of his yard surrounded by cameras and neighbors, he held his old, tattered Bible and explained that he too did not resent the police officers who shot his son but only hoped God would somehow use his son's death for God's purposes.

The video ended and Jose reiterated what we had just witnessed on the video. He also told us the cops who shot his son came to his house later to make sure he did not have a vendetta against them. Apparently they had learned of Jose's violent past and feared he may seek retribution. Jose explained to them that he was a different man now that he had come to know Christ. As Jose ended his talk, he urged the young prisoners in the audience to stop living for themselves and put God first by accepting the grace of Jesus Christ.

Oddly enough, about a month before I heard Jose's testimony, I had the opportunity to hear another man's story which was strikingly similar. Eric had just started coming to our church. I knew I had to go to his side of town to run some errands, so I set up a time to go over his house and visit.

As we sipped our lemonade on his front porch, Eric began to tell me about his views of God. He explained God was there to help him. He was grateful for all the different ways God had revealed himself, how God helped him overcome his addictions, and how God even helped him earn some extra money to buy a new boat.

But then, like Jose, Eric paused. He explained this was not his full testimony, that there was more to his story than just this. Eric's older brother had been involved in a dramatic motorcycle chase with the police some years ago. After the chase, he got off of the motorcycle with a gun and in a blaze of bravado he charged the officers. The group of them unleashed a hail of gunfire leaving any chance of survival completely impossible.

Tragic as it was, like Jose's son, Eric's older brother was also drug induced, armed, and clearly in the wrong. However, Eric's reaction was completely different than Jose's. Eric set out to prove his brother's innocence. He singlehandedly, because no lawyer would help him, tried to accumulate enough evidence to prove the police were at fault for shooting his brother.

He confided in me his deep rage towards the officers overwhelmed him with anger followed by fits of depression and loneliness. As he took me into his house, he showed me a room completely dedicated to proving his brother's innocence. Old newspaper clippings of his brother's case were sprawled all over the desk, as though Eric read them often. Stacked on shelves were large binders filled with crime scene investigations, ballistic results, and numerous other evidence.

Attempt after attempt on Eric's part had failed in court, but he continues to seek retribution for his brother's death. He has been completely consumed by this for years now, and it doesn't seem he will be slowing down anytime soon. It has totally taken over his life.

Why the different reactions? Both men, though it is tragic, clearly made poor choices that forced the police to kill them. Jose was able to move on, but Eric is left reeling in pain. A.W. Tozer said, "What comes into our minds when we think about God is the most important thing about us."[2] I believe the different reactions to similar circumstances happened because of their views of God. One man believed he was there to serve God. The other believed God was there to serve him.

Jose's part one of his testimony explained how God had helped him. Eric's part one of his testimony explained the same. Jose's part two of his testimony, however, explained that even though his son died, he was going to live for God and wanted good to come out of this tragic situation. He equated his happiness with pleasing God, thus could go on in happiness despite the loss of his child. Eric's part two of his testimony had no such details. He had not embraced, as Jose had, that his purpose in life was to serve and worship God no matter what. He was fine when he felt God was helping him, but his problems quickly consumed him when life was no longer turning out the way he thought it should.

Ironically, when we seek personal satisfaction over showing the supremacy of God, we miss accomplishing either; but when his adoration is our highest aim, even over our personal satisfaction, then we experience both.

If He's Supreme I Don't Need to Sell Him

Anyone who works in the ministry will tell you they see stories like Jose's and Eric's all the time. Two people with similar hardships often come out on the other side looking a lot different. I don't fully blame Eric for his view of God. I think he is simply operating out of a system of beliefs he's been taught, like we all do.

Before my eyes began to open to the supremacy of God, when I would tell people about God I was unknowingly giving off the impression that God is in need of us. Often, out of a good desire, Christian leaders try to make your Sunday a repeat experience at their church by satisfying your comforts and wants as much as possible, as though churches are businesses seeking your dollars for the services they provide. They shape the worship, the classes, the preaching, and the whole church environment around what is appealing to you, the consumer.

In short, we often seek to sell God. Though surely done with a motive of love, we seek to make converts through persuasive marketing techniques and proven sales tactics.

When I was doing this, I believe I was subconsciously manifesting the belief that if I was simply used by God to reveal the truth in his word, this would not be enough. Perhaps you've done this. I know I've tried to "sell God." Perhaps you came to Christ like this. And just so we're clear, I do believe someone can genuinely be saved and grow (to some degree) through church encounters like the ones I am describing.

However, if this evangelical sales pitch is all the information a new believer gets about God, his or her life will be extremely confusing and most definitely not as enjoyable as it could be.

One of the most important things anyone can ever know about God is that he is most concerned with the glorification of himself. I'm praying you don't hear me say this with any animosity, but I must say this because I believe it's the truth: God doesn't need us. We need God.

Sometimes I confuse the idea of being a disciple with being a campaign manager. I often think instead of doing his will by following Jesus in an intimate way like a true disciple was made to do, I am actually here to promote God by playing politics. Out of a desire for others to follow, I can be tempted to spin the truth so it appeals to all voters, sometimes spinning it so much it's no longer even the truth. But God isn't running for office because he doesn't need to be elected. He's the one who does the electing. He rules whether people would vote for him or not. He's the Supreme King, not an earthly president.

So on behalf of all the evangelical pitch men and Christian campaign managers out there, I want to apologize for our message. I'm sorry for trying to sell God to you. God doesn't need to be sold. He doesn't sell himself, nor does he hide hard things about himself like a politician trying to improve his poll rating by any means necessary. His word doesn't skirt "controversial" issues revolving around such things as heaven, hell, one path to salvation, all sin deserving death, marriage being between one man and one woman, the futility of faith without works and works without faith, God's election and man's free will, and the list goes on.

As I read through the New Testament Gospels, I am amazed at how differently Jesus sought to make converts compared to our modern tactics. Sure he taught, healed, fed, and was unbelievably kind to people. But he also made it quite clear from the moment people first met him, if they want to follow him, they are going to have to leave everything behind (for some physically but for all spiritually, Luke 18:22); they are going to have to lose their life for him to find life (Matthew 10:39); and by comparison, their love for him should make every other relationship resemble hate (Matthew 10:37). In other words, Jesus made it clear that we are here to magnify God; God is not here to magnify us.

Jesus didn't change his pitch from town to town. He didn't even have a pitch. He simply approached each situation and offered himself, he offered the truth, for he is truth (John 14:6). Jesus is not a chameleon, changing colors to adapt to his surroundings. He is a constant (Hebrews 13:8). People are the variables. He gives people the freedom to love him or hate him, follow him or reject him. All he does is tell the naked truth in the most loving way possible.

Remember the story in John 6 where Jesus fed the five thousand? He had compassion on thousands of hungry people following him, but then he caused nearly all of those people to abandon him by telling them the plain facts (John 6:66), which they did not like: he is the Son of God, the bread of life, and unless they ate his flesh and drank his blood, they would die.

He taught, healed the sick, and casted out demons. Some towns loved him for this and wanted him to stay with them as long as he could (John 4:40). Other towns asked him to leave (Matthew 8:34). Jesus wasn't changing. People's reactions to him were the variables. If people were the point, he would say whatever he needed to in order to get them to follow him, even if it compromised the truth. But he is the point, thus he tells the truth about himself regardless of people's reactions. He does indeed want people to follow him, but followers are not his ultimate aim.

His Ultimate Motivation in All Things

So to start this journey, I would like to talk about God the way Jesus did, with the truth. I'm going to set aside my urges to please my readers, set aside my fear of being misunderstood, my fear of offending people, and just tell you the plainest truth the Bible has to say about God. For the truth is what will bring us freedom, not a pursuit of comfort and self-pleasure. Our greatest problems will not be solved by being warmly loved by a group of well meaning people or by being naively deceived by someone willing to compromise the truth to get us to follow along. Our lives will be radically transformed when we encounter the deep truths of God and embrace them whole heartedly.

And truthfully, if you were to get down to the nitty-gritty motivations behind all that God does, I believe you would discover God does everything ultimately for himself, for his glory. I know it seems counterintuitive when talking about a loving God who died in the place of all sinners, but the Bible makes it very clear that all God does he ultimately does for his own sake. This can be rattling. But it's true nonetheless.

God created everything through himself and for himself (Colossians 1:16). He created the world to declare his glory (Psalm 19:1-4). He formed and made man with the same intent (Isaiah 43:7). He condemns all who dishonor his name (Exodus

20:7), but he also rescues man to bring honor to his name (Jeremiah 14:7, Psalm 25:11). He rescued the Israelites for the sake of his name so he would not be profaned among the nations (Ezekiel 20:9). He parted the waters for them to gain for himself everlasting renown (Isaiah 63:12-14, Psalm 106:8). He placed Pharaoh in leadership to create for himself the opportunity to display his power and so the name of the Lord would be proclaimed in all the earth (Exodus 9:16).

He makes a new covenant with his people, promising them a new heart and spirit, not for their sake but for the sake of his holy name (Ezekiel 36:22-32). He guides us in paths of righteousness for his name sake (Psalm 23:3, Psalm 31:3). He delays his wrath for his own name's sake and for the sake of his praise, and he will not yield his glory to another (Isaiah 48:9-11). For the sake of his righteousness he made his law great and glorious (Isaiah 42:21). He has exalted his name and his word above all things for his praise (Psalm 138:1-2). He blesses people so his ways and saving power may be known among all nations so all nations will praise him (Psalm 67:1-7).

He allows some people to die so he might be glorified (John 11:4). He allows some people to be sick so the power of God may be made known (John 9:3). People are called to obedience by Jesus Christ's power and for his name's sake (Romans 1:5). God saves people so they might live for him (2 Corinthians 5:15, Hebrews 9:14). In everything we do, even in simple things like eating and drinking, we are commanded to do it all for the glory of God (1 Corinthians 10:31). Jesus sought to be glorified so he might glorify his Father (John 17:1). Jesus died on the cross to glorify his Abba (John 12:27-28). The way Jesus blesses his people is by allowing them to see his glory

(John 17:24). And Jesus is the head of the church so that in everything he might have the supremacy (Colossians 1:18).

When we enter his temple, we will yell out, "Glory!" (Psalm 29:9). And when we are living in the New Jerusalem at the renewal of all things, God's glory will replace the sun and be our light forever (Revelations 21:23). There is no doubt, God seeks glory for himself (John 8:50), for from him and through him and for him are all things, so to him be the glory forever! Amen (Romans 11:36).

Clearly, the motivation behind everything God does, even those things that benefit us, are ultimately done to exalt him. God is first and foremost for God. His supreme concern is with himself. His saving works, his grace, his damnation of sinners, his unfailing love – all of it has to do with one thing, him.

God made people out of a desire to glorify himself. If it didn't glorify God to make us, to save us, to love us, he wouldn't have done it. God never ever puts anything above himself. The fact that God made and commands all living creatures to worship him is the very evidence he alone is God.

If he were not absolutely committed to his own adoration, this would point to the fallacy of his claims that he alone deserves worship. If he placed anything above himself he would be breaking his own first commandment, "You shall have no other gods before me" (Exodus 20:3). To legitimize his command for us to place him above all, he must place himself above all as he has told us to do. God's our example in everything, including in exalting God.

God Is Not Prideful. He Is Honest.

God is not being prideful when he states he is the greatest; he's being honest and loving. It would not be humble of God to honor people above himself. It would be catastrophic. God knows the best thing for people is for them to follow and worship him. Since we are all cut off because of our sin, becoming orphaned children, God shows his great love not by sending us a pretty good savior; rather, he sends us the greatest possible Savior ever, himself.

Imagine if a car was flipped over and trapping someone. The car is positioned in such away next to some trees that there is only space for one person to bend down and attempt to tip the car over and off of the trapped victim. Among those watching the horrors is a group of people who look about as equally as strong, except for one obvious choice. His name is Mariusz Pudzianowski, five time winner of the World's Strongest Man Competition, known by some as "The Dominator."

It wouldn't be humble of Mr. Pudzianowski to allow all the bystanders to try and lift the car before him. They may attend the local gym now and then when they know they have a beach vacation coming up, but his strength is on another planet compared to the average person. It would be stupid and unloving for Mr. Pudizanowski to deny his strength for the sake of not hurting people's sensitive egos. The most loving thing he could do would be to tell all those weaklings to step aside and let him flip that car back over like a tin can blowing in the wind. He wouldn't be prideful in doing this; he would be expressing love because he is trying to save that trapped person.

Likewise, God is not being prideful when he tells everyone to step aside and let him be the center of the show. He just knows he is the greatest that has or ever will exist. In honesty and love he tells people to worship him because he knows only he can really do the job of a saving God.

The best thing God could do for me is to make me all about him. His supremacy really does translate into my greatest satisfaction. It would be like if my child needed medical attention. To give my child anything but the best available would be cruel. If I handed my daughter an aspirin when she needs surgery and the surgeon is waiting at my side for my command, this would be incredibly unloving. Being a loving father, I would never do this. So if I, a sinner, can give good gifts to my children, how much more will our Father in heaven give even better gifts (Matthew 7:11).

God wasn't being selfish when he made us for him; he was just giving us the best thing available, the thing better than everything else – himself.

And so here we can already begin to see how God's glory and our good are forever tied together. How would it be good for us if God were no longer God by usurping himself with humans? Secondly, how would it be loving of God to create us for something other than glorifying him if he knows a life centered on him is actually the best life possible?

Yes, we've already begun to cross the line from talking about God's glory to our personal good. In reality, we are not only crossing it, we are discovering there is no line at all. For God's glory and my good are not two separate pursuits but one.

3

The Ultimate Trump Card to Unhappiness

Even suffering will be easier when we are with Him, but without Him, even the greatest pleasures will be joyless. -Brother Lawrence[1]

I said to the Lord, "You are my Lord; apart from you I have no good thing."-Psalm 16:2

"Man!" I blurted out with huff of self-centeredness. We had just gotten done taking our dog out and I was in rush to get back home so I could make it to my next appointment. Living in Cleveland, Ohio, one of the cloudiest and rainiest cities in America, we were trying to take advantage of the rare tolerable weather in the winter months.

But when I was trying to turn left onto my street to get home, much to my chagrin the guy opposite me in the oncoming lane was also trying to turn left. My annoyance meter was rising as we both passively sat staring at one another, wondering if it was clear in the far right lane for us to turn. "This guy is in my way. He's totally blocking my view!"

Bethany, my wife, while filing her nails quietly said in a non-judgmental, factual tone, "He's probably saying the same thing about you."

Bingo. She was totally right. Sitting there, mindlessly attending to the beauty of her finger tips, Bethany had just solved the great mystery of my chronic road rage. My problems stem from my belief that I am the most important person on planet earth. So when someone is blocking my view while I am also blocking his, clearly he is at fault. When I'm late, clearly everyone else is driving too slow and deserves my classic Ballenger-death-stare as I pass them. However, when I have time to kill and feel like practicing my *American Idol* skills to some tunes on the radio, other people are obviously being rude as they speed by giving me their own death-stares. "Jeeze, look at all these speeding sinners," I say to myself in between lyrics. "Why are they rushing me?"

When I realize I am not the center of my own universe, but God is, my anger stemming from self-centeredness is solved. So I am going to be late, is that really what God cares about? Why should I sin against God by losing control of myself because I fear the wrath of my earthly boss if I'm late to work? Did God make me so I could be on time to places or did he make me to glorify him in every situation, even if I'm running late? (Note to all bosses: Obviously God wants us to be on time so we can be good workers. This is not me saying it's okay to be late. It's just an example of solving anger through putting God's glory first. Please, no mean emails.)

Or take my friend Mike for example. Mike has a less than desirable work situation. He is grateful to have a job, but the mundane tasks of his position can be truly grueling. Mike, however, has committed to not being a complainer but rather has embraced his current work situation as an opportunity to honor God by making him his ultimate treasure even when life's circumstances are less than desirable. Mike explains that when he realized his purpose in life was not to have the most amazing job ever but to serve God and enjoy him in every situation he finds himself in, then his work situation suddenly became something much more than mundane. It became the highest calling anyone could ever have – to work in the service of the King. Mike's internal happiness is no longer governed by his external circumstance.

If I were to follow modern wisdom in writing Christian books, this chapter would have come before the previous chapter. That would have been a safer time to hook my readers with how this book will personally benefit them, thus causing them to read further. And I don't believe that would not have been wrong. What's the point of reading a book that doesn't help?

However, for me to have begun explaining how glorifying God benefits you (and it does!) before explaining the truth that God is first and foremost for himself, I would be reinforcing the very mindset that enslaves us and steals our joy in God to begin with. The cure to every discontentment is to live for nothing but the glory of God. When we put our needs and wants (apart from a desire for God) at the center of our pursuits, we are already on the wrong road. Therefore it would not have been helpful to begin you down a road seeking your best life before first explaining the centrality of God's glory.

Every longing is instantly met in our souls when we embrace the truth that God is for God and he made us to center around him in everything we do. When we live as though we are the point, life becomes a fight to prove to everyone, including God, how selfish they are being by not revolving all their time and energies around us. Discontentment simply disappears when we embrace the truth that we are not the point. God is the point, and this is the starting line of the journey to freedom.

Our Joy Is at Stake in Our Decision to Live for Christ's Sake

If anyone knew something about unfavorable external circumstances, it was the Apostle Paul:

> "Five times I received from the Jews the forty lashes minus one. Three times I was beaten with rods, once I was pelted with stones, three times I was shipwrecked, I spent a night and a day in the open sea, I have been constantly on the move. I have been in danger from rivers, in danger from bandits, in danger from my fellow Jews, in danger from Gentiles; in danger in the city, in danger in the country, in danger at sea; and in danger from false believers. I have labored and toiled and have often gone without sleep; I have known hunger and thirst and have often gone without food; I have been cold and naked. Besides everything else, I face daily the pressure of my concern for all the churches." (2 Corinthians 11:25-28)

If anyone had reason to despair and be discontent with life, certainly Paul was this man. However, in just the very next chapter after the above verses and after he describes the weakness he feels because of a thorn in his flesh, Paul wrote something totally profound:

> "Three times I pleaded with the Lord to take [the thorn in my flesh] away from me. But he said to me, 'My grace is sufficient for you, for

my power is made perfect in weakness.'
Therefore I will boast all the more gladly about
my weaknesses, so that Christ's power may rest
on me. That is why, *for Christ's sake*, I delight
in weaknesses, in insults, in hardships, in
persecutions, in difficulties. For when I am
weak, then I am strong." (2 Corinthians 12:8-10,
emphasis mine)

Why was Paul able to live with joy and to even delight in
weaknesses, in insults, in persecutions, and in difficulties? God
did not answer his prayer the way he had originally hoped. God
didn't take away the thorn; he didn't change Paul's external
circumstances. Instead of taking Paul out of a difficult trial,
God used this thorn to teach Paul that happiness in life will not
come through outer pleasures but through finding total joy in
the sufficient grace and power of Jesus Christ.

Paul was able to find his delight even though God did not
remove the bothersome thorn because he was given a new
perspective to view his weaknesses as an opportunity for God
to glorify himself through these weaknesses. Paul now realized
he was to endure all this suffering "for Christ's sake." Because
his new aim was to honor Christ and not himself, he was now
able to find great joy even in personal trials. In 2 Corinthians
4:8-11 he states this truth again:

"We are hard pressed on every side, but not
crushed; perplexed, but not in despair;
persecuted, but not abandoned; struck down, but
not destroyed. We always carry around in our
body the death of Jesus, so that the life of Jesus

> may also be revealed in our body. For we who
> are alive are always being given over to death
> *for Jesus' sake*, so that his life may also be
> revealed in our mortal body."

When I live not for my own sake but "for Jesus' sake," then I truly find my life (Matthew 16:25). Realizing God's pleasure in me is more important than my external circumstances frees me from being controlled by life's ever changing challenges. All of our sins and unhappiness are merely symptoms of the real problem – putting ourselves before God. Solve the root issue and all the symptoms go away as well.

People commit adultery, steal, lie, become angry, avoid confrontation, and sin in every way imaginable simply because we have chosen to live as though we are most important, not God. As Paul explains in 1 Thessalonians 2:4 (ESV), "But just as we have been approved by God to be entrusted with the gospel, so we speak, not to please man, but to please God who tests our hearts."

When God is valued above all else, every discontentment is destroyed.

Pleasure Is Produced Through Fulfilling Your Purpose

Some of you may have noticed that I'm basically just using different words to describe the verses many of us have heard hundreds of times, "If you cling to your life, you will lose it; but if you give up your life for me, you will find it" (Matthew 10:39 NLT). "In all your ways submit to him, and he will make your paths straight" (Proverbs 3:6). "But seek first his kingdom and his righteousness, and all these things will be given to you as well" (Matthew 6:33).

The Bible teaches this truth over and over again: If you put you at the center, life is going to be rather miserable. But if you place God at the center through the power he gives you in Jesus, you will be full of immense joy.

Our satisfaction must be rooted and established in God alone. Sure we can find pleasure in his gifts, but ultimately he should receive the praise even for these. Our internal happiness cannot be sustained by our external circumstances. This isn't to say God will never lead us to switch jobs, get marriage counseling, lose weight, find a different church, or buy a new house. God will lead us to make thousands of changes in our outer worlds as our lives progress with him. But these changes alone will not bring us ultimate joy. Outer circumstance will never be perfect in this age because we live in a fallen world, thus outer circumstances cannot be our primary well of happiness.

Never was this clearer to me than when I had first become a pastor. The job I had while working through seminary was awful. I worked in the basement of a hospital cleaning bloody surgical instruments so they could be sterilized and used again in the operating room. To protect ourselves while decontaminating soiled equipment, we had to wear really uncomfortable protective clothing that did not breathe well at all. The environment was dark, loud because of the cleaning equipment, and the attitude of my coworkers was usually very poor. For eight hours a day I was stuck in what felt like an abyss of boredom, sweat, and other people's blood.

But God was working on me during that time. He was having me recite Scripture in my mind while I cleaned, he had me praying through the long hours of working in solitude, and he was teaching me what it meant to be "content in any and every circumstance" (Philippians 4:12). I can honestly say that despite the dungeon my work environment was, I had many days of joy in Christ there.

Nonetheless, when I was finally hired as a pastor, I was elated. Finally I could provide for my family while also doing work that I enjoyed. What could go wrong? I was working with other Christians, some of whom I had been good friends with for a long time. I was helping people, leading small groups, doing administrative work most Christians would give their right arm to do if they could escape their work place – and yet within just a few months I was seriously considering going back to work at the hospital.

As awesome as it is to work as a pastor, it is still work. For every 50 people that appreciate you, respect you, and are a genuine joy to serve, there is at least one who is the exact opposite. If thirty-five hours a week are spent doing things you enjoy and are good at, there is at least five hours of tasks you are not gifted in and you feel like a failure after doing them. And of course human nature causes us to dwell on the negative, no matter how much good there is too.

As a young, new pastor, I found myself extremely burdened and stressed. But now that I was no longer at the hospital, instead of knowing I had no chance at contentment in the awful circumstance of my job, I felt that since I was now at a church I should be happy since most of my work was not overly burdensome. My good circumstances were tempting me to place my joy in circumstances and not in Christ.

What I learned through this was that I would be happier cleaning blood and guts off surgical instruments if I was finding joy in Christ than if I was not finding joy in Christ but working in a ministry job. Through two very different work experiences, God was driving home the point that no matter what you have in the world to make yourself happy, it isn't going to work. The richest of all men can be miserable, while the poorest of all souls can have amazing joy. All of it depends on understanding and living out the intertwined truth that we are here for God's glory and glorifying God is our good.

Therefore, like Paul, we have the ultimate trump card for whatever troubles may come our way in the phrase "for Christ sake." For Christ sake, I can endure this difficult job. For Christ sake, I can do this work in the church. For Christ sake, I can move on from any ministry when the Lord makes it clear. For Christ sake, I can forgive this wrong. For Christ sake, I can love my spouse in marital trials. For Christ sake, I can accept love from my spouse even when I don't feel I deserve it. For Christ sake, I can raise my kids when they are being ungrateful. For Christ sake, I can seek to please God as a single person. For Christ sake, I can resist this temptation. For Christ sake, I can forgive myself. For Christ sake, I can do his will even when it hurts. "For Christ sake" truly is the ultimate trump card for all of our life's difficulties.

To base your joy in God and not in this world is to no longer be controlled by the uncontrollable ups and downs of a fallen planet. When I accept that the level of my joy is always equivalent to the level of my active love, intimacy, and glorification of God, the conundrum of a joyless life is totally eradicated. This is always true because it's the way God made it. God designed us with his praise as our purpose (Isaiah 43:7). C.S. Lewis explains it this way in *Mere Christianity*:

> "God made us: invented us as a man invents an engine. A car is made to run on petrol (gas), and it would not run properly on anything else. Now God designed the human machine to run on Himself. He Himself is the fuel our spirits were designed to burn, or the food our spirits were designed to feed on. There is no other. That is why it is just no good asking God to make us happy in our own way without bothering about religion. God cannot give us a happiness and peace apart from Himself, because it is not there. There is no such thing."[2]

If you were to fill a car with coffee instead of gas, it wouldn't work. Likewise, when we fill ourselves with earthly pleasures instead of a deep relationship with God, our lives just don't work. He designed us to only be truly happy when we are placing him and his glory first and foremost in our lives.

Even if our outer circumstances are all we dreamed they would be, if God is not being actively enjoyed in our lives through an intimate relationship with him, our internal happiness is still not realized. Out of love God made us for himself because he knew he is the best. He loves us too much to allow us to settle for anything but the best.

We are all sinners from birth (Psalm 51:5), so of course the ways we seek satisfaction have been corrupted. So I don't believe everyone desires to live a godly life. But I do believe every unmet longing in our hearts are actually desires for a life lived for God. Even though most of us try to fill the hole with godless things, in our search for happiness we are all actually searching for him because only he can provide true satisfaction. We keep drinking down mud when what we were made to drink is the purest water available. Is it any wonder why we hurt on the inside?

Since God cares so much about his own glory and our good, he will literally work against our happiness when we are not placing him first in our hearts. God is an all or nothing God. He doesn't want you "sort of happy." He wants you to be fully joyful for eternity. Therefore he wants you to want him because only he brings maximum joy. He doesn't want us drinking less muddy water. He doesn't want us to drink it all; so he keeps allowing us to get sick until we start drinking only what we were made for.

God desires good for me and what is good for me is to glorify God. "This is what the LORD says— your Redeemer, the Holy One of Israel: 'I am the LORD your God, who teaches you what is best for you, who directs you in the way you should go. . . . There is no peace,' says the LORD, 'for the wicked'" (Isaiah 48:17,22). God wants us full of joy and he is trying to tell us that what is going to fill us with the most joy is him. Therefore, the wicked, because the pleasure of God is not their highest aim, have no peace. As Augustine prayed, "You made us for yourself and our hearts find no peace till they rest in you."[3]

You can plug a toaster into an outlet and it will work. Or you can plug it into something else and it will sit useless, never toasting anything. These are the only two options. Likewise, you can't go against God's design and it work out well. You can either embrace your purpose to magnify God and find supreme joy in him, or you can erase your purpose of exalting God and receive the misery of a wasted life. God is a rock. He can either be our firm foundation and our protection, or we can be dashed against him. But he is not moving on this one. He will either make us happy when we are fully his or miserable if we refuse him.

Whether we embrace this truth or not, it is the truth. Isaiah 26:8-9 states, ". . . your name and renown are the desire of our hearts. My soul yearns for you in the night; in the morning my spirit longs for you." We may try to satisfy this desire with other things, which is sin, but our longing for joy will only be satisfied when we make his name and renown the purpose of our existence.

David cried out, "I love the house where you live, O Lord, the place where your glory dwells" (Psalm 26:8). "As the deer pants for streams of water, so my soul pants for you, O God. My soul thirsts for God, for the living God" (Psalm 42:1-2). David knew his desire was a desire only God could quench.

In Psalm 37:4, one of the most quoted verses in the Bible, it reads, "Delight yourself in the Lord and he will give you the desires of your heart." I would argue this is true because the deepest desire of our hearts is to delight in the Lord. When I delight in God my heart's desire, which is to delight in God, is satisfied. I don't believe this verse means because I delight in

God I get the external circumstances I think will make me happy (i.e. the newest technology, the best fashion, marriage, kids, and suburban bliss). Rather because I delight in God my happiness is found because my deepest longing, because God put it there, is to be happy in God.

Sin has corrupted our ability to truly delight in God, therefore we are in need of grace to correct our inability to find satisfaction in him. However, for sinner and saved alike, until we place God at the head of our existence in everything we do through the grace of Christ, the deep desires of our hearts will never be met. When we drink the world's muddy water it just makes us more thirsty, making us drink more and more, progressively sinning in greater and greater shameful ways; but anyone who tastes the living water will never be thirsty again (John 4:13-14).

Therefore, pursuing our best is equivalent to pursuing God.

Back to Center

Up to this point we have discovered God places himself above all things. God is first and foremost for God. His glory is his supreme concern. We have also discovered, however, that God truly does want the best for us. Since he is the best, he makes us for him. To clarify, we have two facts:

1. God is for his glory (Chapter 2).
2. God desires the best for us, which is to glorify him (Chapter 3).

With these two truths, we can discover a third. Since God cares most about his glory and he also desire what is best for us, we can conclude God glorifies himself through doing good for us. If we don't embrace this third fact, there is the temptation to lose focus. Even in our good, God's true agenda is the glorification of himself. This does not taint the authentic good he does. Rather, embracing this truth protects us from making ourselves the center and thus losing the joy that stems from living out our design of magnifying the King. This is now what we have:

1. God is for his glory (Chapter 2).
2. God desires the best for us, which is to glorify him (Chapter 3).
3. Therefore, God must be glorified through our good (Chapter 4).

God desires and orchestrates good for our lives not because we deserve it but because this honors him. He has a vested interest in creating immense good in us, through us, and for us, ultimately for his glory. Our good alone is not the point. To his praise, though, God is glorified through expressing his love to others. His glory and our good are eternally intertwined by his design because of his love.

4

Lifted Up By Coming Down

Since fallen man cannot rediscover and assimilate the form of God, the only way is for God to take the form of man and come to him.-Dietrich Bonhoeffer[1]

The Word became flesh and made his dwelling among us. We have seen his glory, the glory of the one and only Son, who came from the Father, full of grace and truth.-John 1:14

In our world, when someone seeks to exalt themselves, they are usually doing it at the expense of pushing others down. But God is not like this. He's not like kids on a playground.

I remember quite vividly the winter months of elementary school during recess. We would climb the massive snow mounds left by the plow trucks and try to claim the tops for ourselves. You may know this game as "King of the Mountain." We should have referred to it as "Climb the Cleveland Ice Castles Full of Cut Throat Kids."

It may be a little long and not as catchy, but it sure would have been more accurate. Whatever it took to claim the spot of fame at the top, we did it without a second thought. Best friend or not, Nick Sebastian was going down that steep snow mound and hitting every skin scrapping block of ice on his way so he wouldn't even consider crossing me again. And when I was on top, I gloated over all those former friends below . . . until someone blind-sided me as well and I found myself next to Nick, face down in the snow trying to apologize for my betrayal. You see, at recess, just like in our fallen world, the way people get to the top of the mountain is by tossing others off.

Thankfully, though, the God who is love is nothing like the people of the world. People exalt themselves by putting others down. God exalts himself by lifting others up. In fact, check out the way Jesus was exalted:

> [Jesus], being in very nature God,
> did not consider equality with God something to be used to his own advantage;
> rather, he made himself nothing
> by taking the very nature of a servant,
> being made in human likeness.
> And being found in appearance as a man,
> he humbled himself
> by becoming obedient to death—
> even death on a cross!
> Therefore God exalted him to the highest place
> and gave him the name that is above every name,
> that at the name of Jesus every knee should bow,
> in heaven and on earth and under the earth,
> and every tongue acknowledge that Jesus Christ is Lord,
> *to the glory of God the Father.* (Philippians 2:6-11)

Jesus, God himself, came down the mountain and literally died for all of us backstabbing sinners. But he came down to earth not only to save it but to be exalted through saving it.

Jonathan Edwards states, "God in seeking his glory seeks the good of his creatures."[2] God is so amazing, so full of everlasting love and kindness that not only has he placed himself at the center of everything, he has created our reality in such a way that he is exalted best through him producing our good. God pleases himself, which is his highest aim, by being unbelievably lavish and loving towards humans.

Don't Sever Your Lifeline

The temptation after reading the previous chapter about all the good we get when we glorify God is to think the point of glorifying God is our good. If we embrace the lie that God's ultimate motivation in doing us good is simply to do us good, we rob ourselves of the joy only God can give when we lose our life for him.

As Tim Keller explains in his sermon, *The Search for Happiness*, happiness in the Bible is always a bi-product of seeking to honor God more than seeking our own happiness. The Bible never says, "Blessed is he who thirst and hunger for blessedness." It always says the person who is blessed is the one who seeks something greater than their own happiness, something more God honoring (Matthew 5: 3-10). If you seek the worship of God in your life more than personal happiness, you will accomplish both. If you only seek personal happiness and not the worship of God, you will accomplish neither. Notice, the people who are happiest in life are those who have stopped trying so hard to be happy and have begun to live for something greater.[3] As C.S. Lewis stated:

> The woman who makes a dog the center of her
> life loses, in the end, not only her human
> usefulness and dignity but even the proper
> pleasure of dog-keeping. The man who makes
> alcohol his chief good loses not only his job but
> his palate and all power of enjoying the earlier

levels of intoxication. It is a glorious thing to feel for a moment or two that the whole meaning of the universe is summed up in one woman – glorious so long as other duties and pleasures keep tearing you away from her. But clear the decks and so arrange your life that you will have nothing to do but contemplate her, and what happens? Of course this law has been discovered before, but it will stand re-discovery. It may be stated as follows: every preference of a small good to a great, or a partial good to a total good, involves the loss of the small or partial good for which the sacrifice was made.[4]

To search for the good God desires for us but to lose focus of the bigger purpose of glorifying God is to lose everything in the process. If we confuse the order and start elevating our personal satisfaction over our glorification of God, we lose both. The truth is what sets us free. Believing in what God does but rejecting the reasons why he does them robs us of the full truth. Again, as C.S. Lewis explains, "If you look for truth, you may find comfort in the end; if you look for comfort, you will not get either comfort or truth, only soft soap and wishful thinking to begin, and in the end, despair."[5]

If we separate God's motive from his blessings, we lose the true blessing in the process. The cure to our deepest discontentment is to seek our ultimate contentment in magnifying God. If our good becomes the center rather than his glory, we forfeit our good in the process.

We have been thrown a lifeline as we flounder in a sea of self-centeredness. The lifeline is the grace from God to live for pleasing him. When we live from this grace for his glory, God reels us in from the waves of narcissism so we can be free to live above the surface of the selfishness we are drowning in.

But when we think that this lifeline was thrown to us just for us, we are basically taking a sharp knife from our back pocket and severing the very rope pulling us into safety. If we hope to keep grasping this lifeline, this solution to all discontentment, we must realize that even the lifeline, the benefits and blessings God gives us when we glorify him, are actually for him.

When God delivers us, he does it so we can praise him, "Set me free from my prison, that I may praise your name" (Psalm 142:7). Everything, even our good, is actually for his glory.

Praising Him Protects Our Pleasure in Him

God seeking what is best for us is equivalent to him glorifying his own name. He is fiercely committed to the exaltation of his name. Therefore, God is fiercely committed to arranging what is best for us because our good is intertwined with his glorification. When we are blessed by God he is seen as the marvelous, praise deserving King. This deserves jaw dropping awe and wonder when you begin to realize the beauty of our God is expressed best in his blessings.

God's love for us is not tainted even though his ultimate motivation in loving us is to show his beauty. Rather, his love is intensified for us because it is linked to the praise of his name, which is his deepest passion. Words cannot fully describe how awesome and beautiful are the ways of God. The only proper response to such an amazing God is worship.

There's no one like God. No story I could tell, no example I could dream up, no word picture I could make. God is simply God and there is no one as amazing as him. No one could make our reality as good as God has made it.

To drive home the point, read these words of Jesus, "He will bring glory to me by taking from what is mine and making it known to you." (John 16:14). Jesus is glorified when we are benefited. It truly is to our profit when God glorifies himself because he does this most through creating our good. This is why Jesus said in John 16:7, "But I tell you the truth: It is for your good that I am going away."

I've spend this whole book so far explaining that everything God does he does for himself. But now we have Jesus saying he is doing something "for your good." The only way the Bible doesn't contradict itself is if God is glorified through our good. Obviously it would be stupid to dogmatically try and prove Jesus literally does nothing for our good. When he died on the cross and rose from the grave it was good for us. But it was also good for him because when he benefits us through his love, it glorifies him and his Father, which is Jesus' greatest desire.

The author of Hebrews wrote, "Now may the God of peace . . . equip you with everything good for doing his will, and may he work in us what is pleasing to him, through Jesus Christ, to whom be glory forever and ever. Amen" (13:20-21). This pretty well summarizes the interwoven reality of God's pleasure and ours. Let's read it again but this time focusing on how God's glory and our good weave together: "Now may the God of peace . . . equip you with everything good (our good) for doing his will (his glory), and may he work in us (our good) what is pleasing to him (his glory), through Jesus Christ (our good), to whom be glory forever and ever (his glory). Amen" (13:20-21).

The last thing I want to do is preach a health, wealth, and prosperity gospel. But I would be equally as wrong to preach a poverty gospel. No, the gospel does not promise immense earthly wealth or poverty. True saints can be materially poor or rich depending on God's plan. But the gospel does promise immense spiritual riches in Christ Jesus (Ephesians 1:3, 3:14-21).

God wants us all spiritually blessed and rich because it shows how amazing he is. He doesn't want us to die apart from him because it doesn't show anyone how wonderful God's grace is. In Ezekiel 18 it states, "Do I take any pleasure in the death of the wicked? declares the Sovereign LORD. Rather, am I not pleased when they turn from their ways and live? . . . For I take no pleasure in the death of anyone, declares the Sovereign LORD. Repent and live!" (vs. 23,32).

All this is to simply say: Our God is a God deserving of glory. Praising him protects our pleasure in him. It protects our purpose in him. It protects the solution to all discontentment because it centers us on him even when we are being blessed.

My purpose is not to have the perfect job, spouse, kids, vacation, or luxuries. My purpose is not to be lonely, afflicted, hungry, poor, or miserable. My purpose is to please God in every situation at all times. When I worship God in the midst of earthly pleasures, I protect myself from turning these gifts into idols and from receiving the misery accompanied by sin. When I glorify God in my problems, they are no longer problems. They are now working for me and helping me accomplish the thing I want most – the worship of God.

When I adore him, my life is meaningful and full and I am not in danger of severing my lifeline. If I start reveling in myself or my own worth because of all the blessings God has given me, problems arise. The solution to everything is to revolve it all around him. When you revolve anything around anyone, it's called worship. Worship, therefore, enhances the solution because it keeps us God-centered. Even God's blessings are about him. And the more we realize this the more he will bless us.

We Must Be Content "In" Our Circumstances, Not "With" Our Circumstances

I'd like to take a moment and recalibrate. Sometimes to really understand what is being said in the Bible, it helps to define what is not being said. While God wants us to be content in every situation, this does not mean we must become blind to real needs in the world and in our own lives.

To seek an inner tranquility with a total blindness to our actual life circumstances is closer to Buddhism than Christianity. In Buddhism the goal is to reach nirvana, which is a mental state of being that blocks out and ignores the world as you "clear your mind" and focus on nothing. This is not Christianity.

For example, Philippians is a book all about finding joy in Christ despite the external struggles the world throws at us. Throughout the book, you will find Bible verses like these:

> "Whatever happens, conduct yourselves in a manner worthy of the gospel of Christ." (Philippians 1:27)

> "Do everything without grumbling or arguing . . . ." (Philippians 2:14)

> "But even if I am being poured out like a drink offering on the sacrifice and service coming from your faith, I am glad and rejoice with all of you. So you too should be glad and rejoice with me." (Philippians 2:17-18)

> "Finally, my brothers, rejoice in the Lord." (Philippians 3:1)

> "But whatever gain I had, I counted as loss for the sake of Christ. Indeed, I count everything as loss because of the surpassing worth of knowing Christ Jesus my Lord." (Philippians 3:7-8)

> "Rejoice in the Lord always; again I will say, rejoice. . . . Not that I am speaking of being in need, for I have learned in whatever situation I am to be content. I know how to be brought low, and I know how to abound. In any and every circumstance, I have learned the secret of facing plenty and hunger, abundance and need. I can do all things through him who strengthens me." (Philippians 4:4, 11-13)

But even though Paul instructs us to find joy in Christ and not our circumstances, he also has a healthy anxiety over the well being of his coworker who became ill (Philippians 2:25-30).

Even though Paul found that through Christ he had all he needed, he also requested that provisions be made for him by the Philippians (Philippians 4:16-20). And although he learned to find the good in false preachers who still proclaimed Christ (Philippians 1:17-18), he also warned us to stay away from people like that (Romans 16:17-20).

Likewise, Jesus knew that he was going to raise Lazarus from the dead. He knew that it was going to turn out well in the end. But that doesn't mean he didn't weep for Lazarus still. When John 11:35 says, "Jesus wept" it shows us Jesus' perfect humanness. Jesus is God, but he is human too – perfectly both. And thus Jesus cried bitterly in response to the pain of his friends, because to be human is to actually care about things on earth. God really cares about the details of our human lives (1 Peter 5:7), thus to reflect him as image bearers, we must care about the details too. The command to rejoice always is not a command to be a cold hearted robot that pretends pain isn't real.

Again, humans are made in the image of God, and God really cares about the actual circumstances in your life (Matthew 6:8, 32-33). Thus our pursuit of being authentically human reflections of our Creator means we should often time seek to change our external circumstances and bring healing to a broken world. To claim contentment with the world while injustice abounds around you is sin. When society goes wrong, Christians have the obligation to do their best in bringing it back to biblical morality.

Nowhere in the Bible are we told we must enjoy unwanted circumstances. We are told, rather, to enjoy Christ even in unwanted circumstances. You shouldn't be content "with" your singleness (if you want to be married), your low paying job, your broken marriage, your rebellious children, or your divided country. But as a Christ follower whose mission is to glorify the King at all times, we must also be content "in" all these types of trials and circumstances through our relationship with God.

As we've been discussing this whole time, our joy must be found in Christ. No circumstance, no matter how good, will ever fill our hearts' need for God. But there are lesser needs within the heart that God gave humans which are found outside of God himself.

For example, God said of Adam that it was not good for him to be alone (Genesis 2:18), and this was before sin entered the picture. This means that even though Adam had God fully, God still created Adam to need a wife. Eve was never to usurp or challenge God's place in Adam's life. But in love God blessed humans with the opportunity to enjoy symbols and lesser expressions of himself. Therefore, for those who don't have the gift of singleness, it's normal and good to be discontent "with" your singleness, as long as you are content "in" your singleness because you have Christ. Or for those who are married, if your marriage is unhealthy right now, it's normal and good to not be content "with" this. But through Christ, you can be content "in" this dysfunction because Christ is filling you with his love.

So you don't need to feel guilty for wanting certain parts of your life to change and get better. You should only feel guilty and repent if your desires for better life circumstances are crowding out your desire for the Lord. He wants to walk with you through the pain, trials, and unwanted circumstances.

The Christian life can be beautifully summarized by 2 Corinthians 6:10, "we are sorrowful, yet always rejoicing." It's right to not be content "with" your leaky roof, your annoying neighbors, your poor health, or your 80's wardrobe you don't have the money to update. It's a sign of a healthy, alive heart to have levels of sorrow that appropriately correspond to the difficulties in your life, as long as within that same heart you are always rejoicing in Christ.

One Day Our Circumstances Will Match Our Contentment in Christ, but Not Today

Do you remember how we started this chapter? Jesus humbly came to earth to save us and to glorify himself. He came down the mountain because he knew we could never climb it in our own power. He saved us from our sin, thus giving us complete spiritual freedom.

But the story isn't over. God's redemptive act isn't complete. He's going to come again. He still has more glory to bring himself through the renewal of all things. There's always going to be sorrow in the Christians' heart on this earth because we were made for Eden, for a perfect world.

To be content in Christ at all, however, we must first realize the time for a perfect world is not now. If we really think we can make the world whole, refusing to be joyful in Christ until we do, our joy will never be found. In Revelations 21:1-5, John tells us of the future he saw and heard in a vision from God, a future we have yet to attain:

> Then I saw a new heaven and a new earth, for the first heaven and the first earth had passed away, and the sea was no more. [2] And I saw the holy city, new Jerusalem, coming down out of heaven from God, prepared as a bride adorned for her husband. And I heard a loud voice from the throne saying, "Behold, the dwelling place of God is with man. He will dwell with them, and they will be his people, and God himself will be with them

as their God. [4] He will wipe away every tear from their eyes, and death shall be no more, neither shall there be mourning, nor crying, nor pain anymore, for the former things have passed away."

[5] And he who was seated on the throne said, "Behold, I am making all things new."

One day perfect circumstances and perfect contentment in Christ will collide. Should we work to fix this broken planet now? Absolutely. But we must also come to grips with the fact that until Jesus comes and makes all things new, at best we will always be sorrowful because of the pain on this planet while also always rejoicing because of the perfections of our Savior.

When Jesus comes again, we will then be content "with" our outer circumstances and "in" Christ. But before this time comes, we can still find contentment in Christ even with unwanted circumstances.

5

Enhance the Effect By Clarifying the Cause

A man can no more diminish God's glory by refusing to worship Him than a lunatic can put out the sun by scribbling the word, 'darkness' on the walls of his cell. -C.S. Lewis[1]

And I will give them one heart and one purpose: to worship me forever, for their own good and for the good of all their descendants. - Jeremiah 32:39 (NLT)

When my son was a baby and he had a dirty diaper, we cleaned him because we loved him. We didn't love him because he was clean. If this would have been the case, my son would have basically received love about three percent of his childhood.

Right from the start the boy was just plain messy. I remember when we took him home from the hospital and I got to change his diaper for the first time. Bethany was there to supervise because, like most men, I had never changed a diaper until I had a kid of my own.

Well, unbeknownst to me, he was still getting rid of his meconium. If you've never had a baby, this is the fancy word for the baby's poop they have for the first few days of life out of the womb. If you've never seen it, imagine rotting brownie batter mixed with tar and you will have a fairly accurate picture. It's nasty, to say the least.

As I attempted to change him, the meconium had overwhelmed the defenses of his diaper. Then I panicked and tried to shove the diaper down the "Baby Genie," a horrible invention with a narrow opening meant to dispose of stinky diapers while keeping the smell in. When I hastily shoved the diaper through the narrow opening of the Baby Genie, the meconium oozed out onto my hand and dripped on the floor.

I would be lying if I said the sight of meconium on my hand didn't add to my growing terror. (Remember, I was a rookie then; I would scoff at a little meconium on my hand now.) To make matters worse, my dog and her perverted appetite decided to try and lick the drops of meconium off the floor. And if this was not enough, as I was trying to kick the dog away from fulfilling her twisted desire to eat this toxic liquid poop and before I could get the new diaper securely fitted, my new bundle of joy decided he needed to pee. A steady stream arched into the air.

Over the hysterical laughter of my wife as I dodged my son's water works directed my way, I wondered aloud how it was possible to change a baby's diaper without a team of highly trained Navy Seals. I'd like to say once the meconium stage was over things got a little easier, but that would not be true. His next memorable strike involved my wife, thankfully (but don't tell her I said that).

As I came down from my home office and went into my son's room, I found my opportunity to return the laughter my wife paid me. As I looked closer at the scene before me, Bethany had puke in her hair, pee on her shirt, and she was holding another defeated diaper that had no chance against my son's massive baby blowout. Realizing my son needed to know how much we did for him as a baby, before Bethany had the chance to clean him and herself I snapped a picture to capture this moment for years to come.

As a young dad I learned quite quickly: parents don't love their kids because they are clean. Parents clean their kids because they love them. And that's how God loves us. We are constantly messing ourselves with sin but God continues to clean us through the grace of Jesus because it is within him to do it. He does not love us because we are clean of sin. He cleans us of sin because he loves us.

The truth is that God is fully glorious and loving with or without humans worshipping him. Clarifying the source of his glorious attributes enhances the solutions they bring to our problems.

God Is the Cause of the Cure

In the last chapter, we discovered God has thrown us a lifeline by giving us the chance through Christ to live for him. Living for his glory saves us from the deep, dangerous sea of me-centered living. But when we start to believe he threw the lifeline just for our good and not also for his glory, we sever it because we put ourselves back at the center.

We must also notice one more thing about this lifeline if we hope to keep it firmly in our grasp as we are reeled in: God threw it. It sounds rather silly to point out, but if you are drowning and you're the only one around to throw a lifeline . . . you're going to drown. Profound, I know. However, to embrace the cure produced by glorifying God, we must realize the source of his glory.

If the sun only shined when people enjoyed it, we would never get the chance to enjoy it in the first place. For the sun's rays to shine and bring me joy in them, they must be the cause of my joy, not the effect. If my joy in the brightness of the sun was what caused the brightness, this would be a very dark and joyless world.

Likewise, God's worth is not dependent upon me. God is not in need of people like we are his batteries. If I were God's battery, we would both be empty because God fills me, not the other way around. If light was only produced by my ability to see in the dark, then I would be forever blind. The light is what causes me to see. My sight is not what causes the light. God must be the cause, the cure, the perfect light, or else he and I are both doomed. He fills me, I can't fill him.

Anyone who's married knows this principle firsthand. When I first got married to Bethany, we both realized pretty quickly neither of us were very good at filling the other person. Like many young newlyweds, we had visions of being crazy happy all the time because we would finally be together the way we couldn't be when we were unmarried. No more going home, no more not sleeping in the same bed, no more talking on the phone so much. But a few months after the honeymoon, when real life began to soak in, we had to wake up. We would both come home tired from work, school, and the pressures of daily life. When we went to each other to make ourselves feel better, it was like one empty battery trying to fill the other.

We certainly still fall back into this faulty thinking sometimes, but over the years we've really learned to enjoy each other more and more because we are seeking our ultimate happiness from one another less and less. Marriage is amazing, my wife is my best friend, but a spouse, along with every other gift God gives us, is no substitute for God because only he is fully stable and in need of nothing to fill him.

God is glorious to the max, stable forever, and totally fulfilled in himself. God doesn't need us. Although this can come as a shock, it should also come as our greatest relief.

The Cause of God's Glory Is God

In the midst of seeking to reveal that the cure to internal discontentment is to live to please God all the time, I've been throwing around the terms "God's glory" and "glorifying God" pretty heavily. Words are worthless, however, if we don't remember their meanings. Max Lucado in *It's Not About Me* gives a great explanation of God's glory:

> What the word Alps does for the mountains of Europe, glory does for God's nature. Alps encompass a host of beauties: creeks, peaks, falling leaves, running elk. To ask to see the Alps is to ask to see it all. To see God's glory is to ask to see all of God. God's glory carries the full weight of his attributes: his love, his character, his strength, and on and on.[2]

Additionally, when I use the words "glorifying God," I mean it like it is used in Romans 1:21 (NIV), "For although they knew God, they neither *glorified* him as God nor gave thanks to him . . . ." The word "glorified" here is the same Greek word used in 2 Thessalonians 3:1 (NIV) for "honored," "Finally, brothers, pray for us that the message of the Lord may spread rapidly and be *honored* . . . ." Therefore, when I say we are to "glorify God" or "bring him glory," I mean we are to honor him as he deserves, reflect him as we were made to do, make much of him in every way, make his character known to the world, and worship him in our personal lives. What I don't mean when I say "glorify God" is that God's glory is somehow dependent upon us giving it to him.

With a poor understanding of these words, the great temptation in all of this is to fall into the lie that since God commands us to worship him, he must be in need of our worship. Thankfully, God is unfathomably majestic and supremely splendid whether we glorify him or not.

He is fully sufficient, stable, and happy within himself. A.W. Tozer put it like this, "If every man on earth became blind, it would not diminish the glory of the sun and the moon and the stars. And if every person on earth turned atheist, it would not diminish the glory of God."[3] God is constant, never changing, and thus he is the only one we should truly and fully rely on.

So when we read in places like Psalm 34:3 that we are to "glorify the Lord" and "exalt his name," it does not mean we actually add to the greatness of our Lord. That is totally impossible. But it does mean that God is concerned that his importance be highlighted in our personal lives. In Psalm 66:2 it says to "make his praise glorious!" We can make his praise glorious, but he is glorious whether we praise him or not. He won't be joyful with our personal lives if we don't praise him, but he is maximally joyful and glorious all the time within himself.

All this raises the question: If God doesn't need us to praise and please him, why does he command us to do it?

The Effect of Glorifying God Benefits Us

I don't claim to fully understand why God does what he does, but I believe the truths in the Bible give us some answers here. The most obvious reason God commands us to glorify him is because he deserves it. 1 Chronicles 16:29 (NLT), "Give to the LORD the glory he deserves!"

As we have already discussed, God also commands us to glorify him because it would have been cruel of him not to. Since God is love, he always does what it most loving. If he were to make us for something lesser than himself, that would not have been very loving because we would then be missing out on what is best, which is him. Therefore, perhaps God commands us to glorify him not because he needs it but because he knows we do. Jeremiah 32:39-41 (NLT) explains:

> And I will give them one heart and one purpose: to worship me forever, for their own good and for the good of all their descendants. And I will make an everlasting covenant with them: I will never stop doing good for them. I will put a desire in their hearts to worship me, and they will never leave me. I will find joy doing good for them . . . .

When God saves us through the gospel of Jesus Christ, he puts a desire in our hearts to worship him not because he needs our worship but because this is what is good for us. And remember, God glorifies himself through our good ("I will find joy in doing good for them . . .") so this does not put us at the center of all things.

God expresses his goodness and love by commanding us to praise him, "Give thanks to the Lord, *for he is good*, his love endures forever" (1 Chronicles 16:34). It clearly states that "God is good, his love endures forever" meaning his goodness is a permanent state of existence that is rooted within himself, not in who we are or what we do. We are to praise him not to make him good but because he already is.

God's love for people is dependent upon God. God is good regardless of our response to him. Our sins do not change God; rather our sins change our ability to enjoy him and receive his blessings. God does not need our glorification, but he commands it of us because he knows our participation in his praise will be our greatest pleasure.

Clarifying the cause of God's glory will enhance the effect it has on us. Knowing he is completely content and glorious in himself with or without us should increase our understanding of his love for us, not diminish it. We are not needed by him. We are not some battery he uses to charge himself. We are not integral to who God is.

Yes he finds delight in us. Yes he is pleased with our actions at times. But he is still always satisfied and full of joy regardless of us. Therefore we can be confident of his love even when our love for him fails. We can trust his forgiveness because his faithfulness is based in him, not in our sinlessness. He didn't create us because he needed us. It was simply the natural response of a totally pure love to create others to share in that love.

It's like a healthy marriage. The two are happy with one another and love each other, and the natural response of this type of loves is to expand and spread. So the couple has children. They do this not because they need the kids to be happy or want to use them for selfish gain. They desire to have children because they simply want to allow other people to share in their love. Love always creates life.

Marriages, however, that have children hoping kids will make everything better end up smothering their children or spoiling them because the parents demand the kids give what the they were never designed to give – fullness of joy.

This creates rotten children because they feel they are the center of the universe. They either embrace this role and become self-exalting, or they resent this role and become bitter. Parents who do this tear their kids apart because they seek to take from their children rather than give to them. God is the best parent around. He creates the healthiest kids because he is not going to them because he needs their love but rather because he is full of love to give. He loves them because he is love and it expresses his glory to do so.

Only God Needs Nothing, So Only God Can Give Everything

God does not love us because of what we do, he loves us because of who he is, for "God is love" (1 John 4:8). This means God's love is never wavering. It wasn't given to us because of something we've done, therefore it will never be taken away by something we might do.

When we turn from God and sin, God's heart breaks for us, not for himself. God is not in heaven constantly getting his feelings hurt. But he is saddened when we turn from him. Not for himself, but for us (Jeremiah 2:19). He yearns for a relationship with us not because he needs it but because he understands our needs and how lost we are without him. He knows that everything is solved for us when we live for nothing but him because nothing but God is fully stable.

He is honored, magnified, and exalted through our relationship with him, but not in a way where things are added, only revealed. We should take great comfort in God's steadfast love that is based within himself and not in us. We must realize that we can never really let the love of God down because we were never the ones holding it up. As Piper explains in *God's Passion for His Glory*, "The basic movement of worship on Sunday morning is not to come with our hands full to give to God, as though he needed anything, but to come with our hands empty, to receive from God."[4] This type of worship honors him much more.

Psalm 50:12 states, "If I were hungry I would not tell you, for the world is mine, and all that is in it." Acts 17:25 says, "And he is not served by human hands, as if he needed anything. Rather, he himself gives everyone life and breath and everything else." This shouldn't be a sad thing. I thank God that he doesn't need me. If God needed me, who would I go to when I am in need? And in Scripture if it does appear at times that God needs us, C.S. Lewis explains, "If He who in Himself can lack nothing chooses to need us, it is because we need to be needed."[5]

Have you ever really thought about John 3:16? "For God so loved the world that he gave his one and only Son, that whoever believes in him shall not perish but have eternal life." God loved the world? The world is a disgusting place. It is full of people who were born totally depraved (Psalm 51:5). It is overflowing with rapists, murders, child molesters, thieves, liars and "common" sinners like you and I who are just as deserving of hell as the rest of the bunch. And God loved it? Why? He didn't see some glimmer of hope in us (Romans 5:8, 1 Corinthians 5:10, 1 John 2:16). He didn't see something beautiful he just had to save. He loves us despite of us. He loves because he is full of love.

At the peak of human insult towards Jesus during the crucifixion, he prayed, "Father, forgive them, for they do not know what they are doing" (Luke 23:34). He could pray with love towards those who were literally killing him because his love is not contingent upon them at all. God's unchanging nature is the source of our existence, our salvation, and all of our joy because it means he will never break his covenant, never abandon us once we are truly saved. Again, as Lewis explains, "The great thing to remember is that, though our feelings come and go, God's love for us does not. It is not wearied by our sins, or our indifference; and, therefore, it is quite relentless in its determination that we shall be cured of those sins, at whatever cost to us, at whatever cost to Him."[6]

The instability of my joy is solved when I live to please God because only he is totally unchanging and stable forever. He is the only one truly secure in himself, therefore only he can give us the perfect security and love we desire.

6

Take the Highest Bid

Your connection with Calvary is the most important thing about you. . . . When you reach the upper realms your most important memory will not be that you were wealthy or poor in this life, nor the fact that you sickened and died, but that you were "bought with a price." -Charles Spurgeon[1]

Soon they became vile, as vile as the god they worshiped. - Hosea 9:10 (NLT)

My best friend, Scott, is a Craigslist junkie. He is constantly buying old stuff and then flipping it for a profit. Every now and then I will go with him to do a deal. If any of you are familiar with the world of collectors, which is often the same world the hoarders live in, you know many of these people are a little on the crazy side. Their houses are full of trash they think is treasure and they get rather mad if you accidently break their things, such as an antique fish tank . . . but that's another story.

Scott will go through their garbage with a fanatical glint of excitement in his eyes as if he was searching through piles of dirty diamonds in need of just a little dusting off. As he's rummaging knee deep in the junk of someone we just met, I'll be off in the corner tucking my pants into my socks so nothing can crawl in.

I remember one time he bought a box of old Atari video games. I, as usual when I come along for his charades, mocked him relentlessly for his insane vision of actually flipping them for a profit. Who would pay money for video games as old and boring as your grandparent's puzzle collection?

As usual, however, he went against my practical words of wisdom, and, oddly enough, as usual, he made a significant profit – a thousand bucks to be exact! You see, I am a horrible flipper because all I ever see is broken-down, worn-out junk. Whenever I tag along with him our conversations go something like this: "Dude," because when I hang out with my best friend I instantly get transported back into 1995, "how much do you really think this junk you just bought is actually worth?"

Undaunted by my negativity, Scott responds quite calmly and with a small grin he knows will annoy me, "Things are worth whatever people will pay for them, Mark." And that's his secret to being a good flipper.

He can resell junk for a profit because he knows the value of something is dependent upon how much people will pay. I see things for the value they actually are as they stand by themselves. But Scott sees through the eyes of his buyer. He knows value is not dependent upon the stuff, it is dependent upon the people who are paying for the stuff. And he knows his buyers have some seriously deep pockets.

I remember watching a documentary that proved this idea once again. It chronicled a sports fan's fanatical obsession with raising enough money to buy the original document the rules of the game of basketball were written on by the creator of the sport, James Naismith. James Naismith was a gym teacher who created the game of basketball and then pinned the rules up on the wall for all to understand how the game was to be played.

Now over one hundred years later and with basketball being a global, billion dollar sport, the price at auction for these pieces of paper topped 4 million dollars!

Throughout the documentary I was talking to the TV as if Scott were there gold panning through piles of garbage. "Dude, come-on, how much can these old, tattered pieces of paper really be worth? I can go to Office Max right now and get some brand new paper for a few bucks. Dude, don't waste your money. Dude . . . please, this is ridiculous."

There I was again, making the same mistake. At the end of the movie when the guy had raised over 4 million to get the documents, I felt like Scott was there smiling back at me with that grin of his, "Things are worth what someone will pay for them, Mark." As confusing as this is to me, Scott seems to have a point.

And this is how it is in the Christian life. Our value is not simply based on our worth by ourselves. Rather we our worth whatever someone will pay for us. And since Jesus has already paid the highest price for us – himself on the cross – we would be fools to not accept this deal and receive this immense worth.

Our Value Is Based on Who Buys Us

We are constantly trying to create worth in ourselves by our works. We often think God values and loves us because of what we bring to the table. We think God chooses and elects us because he saw something special in us. But none of this is true. When God looks at people apart from the grace of Jesus Christ, he doesn't see potential, he sees a problem.

And yet he truly does love us immensely, more than we can ever fully know. As we discussed in the previous chapter, the only reason God can love us even though we were his enemies is because his love is not based in us at all. He does not love us because of what we do. He loves us because of who he is. If this is true, we must also then realize our worth is contingent upon the things we are worshipping.

Jeremiah 2:5 states, "What fault did your fathers find in me, that they strayed so far from me? They followed worthless idols and became worthless themselves." My worth is equal to whom I worship not because I earn my value through my worship. Rather, my worth is equal to whom I worship because love is not found in what I do but in the nature of the God, or gods, I serve. And as we can see from the verse above, there is no fault in God so only he can give a perfect love; therefore, it would make sense that we should seek to live for him alone rather than for other faulty gods who have nothing to give us.

Love is always given, not earned. If you earned it, it is something other than true love. God loves because he is love. Since idols are worthless and have no true love to give within them, when I worship them rather than God, I only have what they give me, which is nothing. People will be living a worthless life when God is not the one they seek to serve because God is the only one with any worth to give.

When Christians do not actively try to please God, they will *feel* worthless because their intimate relationship with God will be hindered. Sinning is cutting yourself off from the endless relational fountain of value – God himself.

Living in this world is like being an item in an auction. As we stand up and look out, there are tons of bidders yelling and competing to buy us. In an auction, though, the item does not go to the loudest yeller. It always goes to the highest bidder because the seller logically always wants the most return on the sale.

When it comes to living in this world, however, people don't always take the best price for themselves. Idols yell at us like people in an auction, seeking to drown out the voice of God, promising us things they can never actually pay. But since God is the richest, he always has the highest bid out for us, and he alone can actually follow through with his promises since he already paid the ultimate price with the blood of Christ. Like a seller in an auction, we should obviously go with the highest bidder, not the loudest bidder. As 1 Corinthians 6:19-20 (ESV) explains, "You are not your own, for you were bought with a price. So glorify God in your body."

Jeremiah 2:11 in the ESV states, "But my people have changed *their glory* for that which *does not profit*." In the NIV it reads, "But my people have exchanged *their glorious God* for *worthless idols*." When we look at these translations together, we can see the meaning of this verse is that God is the peoples' glory. When they stopped worshipping him, they stopped benefitting themselves, they stopped being glorious. They lost their value because they exchanged "their glory (ESV)," which is their "glorious God (NIV)," for "that which does not profit (ESV)," which is "worthless idols (NIV)."

We only have the highest value when we are God's because only he has any value and love to give. Worthless idols do not benefit us because they have no worth to give. If you want to feel valuable and loved, then commit your life to glorifying God. An intimate relationship with Jesus fills like nothing else because God is full of love to give like no one else.

Making Me Look So Good Makes Him Look the Best

Some people argue me on this and say God loves us and we are valuable because we are made in his image. I agree it is important to understand every person is made in the image of God. Because of this everyone is entitled to certain rights, respect, and safeties as human beings living on this shared earth.

However, I don't believe God loves us *because* we are made in his image. I believe we are made in his image because he loves us. If God loves us mainly because we are made in his image that would mean he would have to love us less now that sin has tainted that image. God loves because he is full of unfailing love and he chooses to do so. I believe God loves us, *therefore* he made us in his image.

Our image bearing is not the cause of God's love, it is the effect. The result of his love is he made us look like him. God knows he is the most beautiful, therefore, since he loves us, he wanted to make us bear the image of the most beautiful person around; and since he loves us, he seeks to restore the broken image through the work of Jesus Christ. Our image bearing was not meant to make much of us. It benefits us, but it does not exalt us. Rather, it makes much of him.

When I wear a jersey of my favorite sports player, I'm not the one getting exalted; the person's name I am bearing gets the glory. I may look really good wearing their jersey and find joy in the way I look. But the athlete whose jersey I am wearing deserves the praise for this, not me. Likewise, even though I am wearing God's image and I look and feel really good doing it, God deserves the worship, not me. Even our image bearing of him points to the truth that God's glory is what he is most about. God is the real star. We're simply wearing his jersey and enjoying the benefits of it.

Jeremiah 2:32 states, "Does a maiden forget her jewelry, a bride her wedding ornaments? Yet my people have forgotten me, days without number." Like jewelry to a bride, God is to us. The thing that makes us beautiful is our God. As C.S. Lewis put it, "For the Church has not beauty but what the Bride-groom gives her; he does not find, but makes her lovely."[2]

He gives us worth, strength, and the power to experience our greatest good which is his glorification in our lives. That's why in Jeremiah 2:19 God says, "Your wickedness will punish *you*; your backsliding will rebuke you. Consider then and realize how evil and bitter it is for *you* when you forsake the LORD your God and have no awe of me,' declares the Lord, the LORD Almighty."

God points out the person who is truly hurt by our lack of worshipping him is not God but the person who lacks worshipping him, the person who runs from their true calling in life. He is saddened for us, he is emotionally hurt for us; but ultimately we are hurt, not God, when we do not stand in awe of the Lord.

Jeremiah 2:37 ends the chapter with the grim warning to the Israelites, "You will be disappointed by Egypt as you were by Assyria . . . for the Lord has rejected those you trust; you will not be helped by them." In other words, when we put our hope in anything other than in God, we will be left unfulfilled and depressed because only God has true power and thus only he has the ability to fill us with sustained joy.

You will always doubt your worth and value as an individual when you doubt the unchanging nature and glory of God. If you think God is unstable, you will always doubt the sustainability of the gifts he gives you. You will always call into question your cleanness and your value until you realize how fixed God is. Our power is equal to the one we praise. He gives us love, he gives us worth, and he gives us our "daily bread" (everything we need daily) because he is full of these things to give. He doesn't give them because we deserve them, and he won't take them away because we don't deserve them.

If our daily god is TV, coffee, and human relationships, these things will disappoint us because they are not fully glorious as God is. But when God is not just our god in theory but the one we go to every moment of the day, then we are given the power we need to do what pleases him and benefits us.

God knows it is best for us to glorify him because he knows only he has any real value to give. Value and power are things that are given to us by the God, or gods, we serve. When we worship other gods we become worthless and powerless because they are worthless and powerless (Psalm 115:8). When we worship God, he gives us value and power because it is in him to do so. We should not seek to be found worthy because of our works; rather, we should seek to worship God because of the worth he freely and undeservedly already placed on us because of what Jesus has done.

We may not always understand everything that happens to us, but we can always know God loves us and values us because that's the type of God he is. He will never change. Even though life is full of ups and downs, God is stable all the time.

7

Our Mess Can Be His Miracle

It is doubtful whether God can bless a man greatly until He has hurt him deeply. -A.W. Tozer[1]

For our light and momentary troubles are achieving for us an eternal glory that far outweighs them all. -2 Corinthians 4:17

Everything changed for me when I was in the fourth grade. I remember my mom had picked up my sister and me from school as she normally did. As we drove home, she seemed a little quieter than normal, but we really didn't think much of it at the time. When we walked into the house, she immediately told us to sit down on the couch because she had something to tell us.

Subconsciously I knew this wasn't one of those talks we got for doing something wrong. Her voice had a different tone to it than when she gave us her motherly lectures I had heard so many times before. Nevertheless, I started to feel that sinking sensation in my stomach I used to get when I would forget to do that big project my teacher had been telling me about for months.

"You're dad is in the hospital. He's had a massive stroke." As soon as she said the words, she burst into tears. I had no idea what a stroke meant, but from the immediate horror that came over my older sister and from the sobs of my mom over her divorced husband, I knew it had to be serious.

As the coming days went by, vivid memories burned into my mind. I remember walking to the Intensive Care Unit for the first time and seeing my dad lying lifelessly in bed, mumbling incoherently from time to time. I remember being upset over the little things the hospital staff was doing to him, like how they would only allow him to hydrate through an IV and wet his mouth a few times a day through sponges and ice chips. They explained they were doing this so he wouldn't have anything to vomit and possibly choke on, but I didn't care as boy. Things that seemed cruel but that were actually for my dad's good still just seemed cruel through my young eyes.

Staring out the glass window dividing the hallway and the waiting room, I saw them rush him to the operating room to perform emergency surgery the doctor warned had a high chance of failure. They took half of his skull out to make room for his swelling brain, and to the amazement of the hospital staff, it worked.

When I came to visit after school a few days later, my dad was sitting up in bed with family and friends smiling around him. But my joy turned to confusion once I looked closer at him. He was no longer the dad I once knew. Due to the brain damage everything changed for him. Physically, emotionally, mentally, and even relationally – it was all difficult and different now.

To a young boy who had idolized his dad as Superman, my dad's wounds were now my wounds. If the rock of our family could go down, what is really stable in this world? What isn't at risk? Through the years, we all began to realize, my dad included, that who he was before the stroke was no more. The "old dad" had died. As the years went by, my new dad would prove just as loving and supportive as the other. But I would be lying if I said this incident didn't shape nearly my entire outlook on life and God in the years to follow.

Sunday school and religion class at the Christian academy I attended had drilled into my mind that God was good and loving. But why did this happen then? Why did God allow me so much pain as a child? Couldn't God have taught me the lessons I learned through this in a less hurtful way? Did he cause this to happen or did he merely allow it?

Years later and now with a wealth of experience proving God's faithfulness, I'm still not sure I have answers to all of these questions. Perhaps what I have learned is that these are the wrong questions to be asking.

Only God Defines Our Good

In the last chapter we learned that God is good all the time. However, when we look at our external lives, this doesn't always seem to be clear to us. If God is good all the time, why did you just lose your job? Why did my dad have a massive stroke when I needed him most? Why is your marriage falling apart? Why do parents get divorced? Why do you have to sit in traffic every day? Why are there so many annoying problems in the world, like traffic? And why is life just so dang difficult?

I think the answer lies in our definition of "good." When I have been writing that "God is glorified through our good," I don't mean he is glorified through our various definitions of what each one of us consider good. You may consider it good to be rich and famous; I may want to live in a hole with no one to bother me, yelling at the neighbor kids who run on my grass outside my hole.

We cannot use our personalized definitions of "good." If we do, we will always doubt God's heart for us because we will constantly be interpreting life's difficult circumstances as God's lack of love. We must use his definition of what is "good" for us. And his definition has less to do with our outer circumstances and more to do with our inner transformation and ability to honor him.

God being glorified through our good does not mean I should expect him to be my personal genie. C.S. Lewis explains, "Love is not affectionate feelings, but a steady wish for the loved person's ultimate good as far as it can be obtained."[2] God knows the best thing for me is to worship him; therefore, he will constantly be working and arranging my life so this happens, no matter the short-term consequences.

So what is our ultimate "good?" Our good is it to glorify God and to enjoy his supreme glory in everything. It can come from life or death, but God will allow whatever circumstance he needs for his name to be most magnified in our lives. We may not always understand his grand plan on this side of eternity, but we can trust everything he does will benefit us because everything he does is meant to glorify him.

Without a Death Their Can't Be a Resurrection

Our pain is our gain when grace is applied because it is God's opportunity to display his power in our lives. Never in the Bible is there a miracle without a mess. Jesus never heals anyone who isn't first sick. He never quiets calm waters. He never produces food for people who already have enough. God always displays his glory in a miraculous way by first allowing a massive problem to arise. He doesn't do miracles for entertainment purposes or to produce tingles on our necks. His purpose is always to display the power of Jesus to save.

God loves us so much that he allows short-term pain in our lives to display his glory which then produces long-term joy. I think this is what Jesus was trying to teach us through the raising of Lazarus:

> 3 So the sisters [Mary and Martha] sent word to Jesus, "Lord, the one you love is sick."
>
> 4 When he heard this, Jesus said, "This sickness will not end in death. No, it is for God's glory so that God's Son may be glorified through it."
> 5 Now Jesus loved Martha and her sister and Lazarus. 6 So when he heard that Lazarus was sick, he stayed where he was two more days.
> (John 11:3-6)

To most of us, the phrase "the one you love is sick" seems like an oxymoron. If Jesus loves Lazarus, why the heck is he sick? We naturally associate easy external circumstances with God's pleasure towards us and hard external circumstances with God's displeasure towards us.

Christians often view God like I viewed the hospital staff as a little child. I couldn't see that the short-term displeasure the doctors and nurses were causing my dad with their treatments was actually meant for his long-term good. As a young boy I thought they were just mean because I could not see the bigger picture. Not until years later when I was grown and enjoying the company of my dad did I begin to realize what seemed like cruelty was actually done to save his life. God often treats us the same way. He will do whatever it takes to save us from death, even if it means sacrificing our short-term comforts (Hebrews 12:6).

Likewise, Jesus allowed Lazarus to be sick *because* he loved him. Notice in verse 5 it clearly states Jesus loved the sisters and Lazarus. Then verse 6 explains with extreme clarity (notice the word "So") how Jesus expresses that love. He purposely waits two more days so that Lazarus dies. Jesus shows his love not by keeping them from pain, but by allowing pain so he could use it to magnify himself in their lives. Jesus knew it was better for them that they experience his greatness and know he is God rather than to spare them of short-term displeasures. He knew if he didn't allow a death in the family, he would never have a chance to produce a resurrection.

Jesus knew the darker the situation got, the brighter his glory would shine for those he sought to express his affection. He didn't just want them to love him with an average love. He wanted to produce in them a deeper awe of his greatness than they had ever known. Because Jesus did not spare them of short-term difficulties, they gained a lavish love for Jesus they wouldn't have otherwise had.

In John 12 we see the family throwing a party for Jesus. Mary takes out the rare perfume worth a year's wages and pours it on Jesus feet and then wipes his feet with her hair. Mary is the one who performs this act of love, but I bet the whole family was in it on it. No one in the family objected, and Martha was not shy about voicing her complaints (Luke 10:40). Mary, Martha, and Lazarus I'm sure were all overjoyed to spill a year's wages on the feet of Jesus. But I wonder if they would have been so lavish if they hadn't just witnessed Jesus raising Lazarus from the dead in John 11?

I think this is what Jesus is trying to do all the time. He allows messes to form in our lives so he has an opportunity to produce miracles. He doesn't just want our average love; he wants lavish love like Mary showed. This type of love in us can only be produced when we allow Jesus to finish what he started.

It would have been really simple for everyone to start doubting Jesus once Lazarus died. Jesus said in John 11:4, "This sickness will not end in death. No, it is for God's glory, so that God's Son may be glorified through it." If I were there, I would have assumed this meant Lazarus was *not* going to die. But that's not what Jesus said. He said this tragedy will not "end" in death. He didn't say Lazarus wasn't going to experience death. How often do we mistake the promises of God in similar ways?

The easy thing to do would have been to throw their hands up and gripe at Jesus. The hard thing, the thing that eventually produced immense joy in them, was to trust that even though life wasn't working out the way they thought it should, Jesus can turn any death into a resurrection if we allow him to finish what he intended from the start.

Don't Stop the Artist Halfway Through His Masterpiece

Jesus was the only one in this story who knew the end result. He had a plan from the beginning of what he wanted to do. He didn't forget to set his alarm clock and accidentally allowed Lazarus to die. He didn't get stuck in the morning rush hour commute on his way to the city of Bethany where Lazarus lived. It wasn't as though Jesus didn't care enough to save Lazarus but then raised him from the dead because he felt bad after seeing everyone crying. Jesus had a plan, but the people had to stick around long enough to allow him to finish what he started in order to witness his faithfulness.

So often when we hear that God is faithful, we assume his faithfulness will translate into an easy and clean life. When we experience a job loss, a church split, a health scare, a divorce, or some disappointment in life, we naturally assume God is not as loving as we hoped. But God never promised we wouldn't die if we trust him. He just said that our stories would not end in death. The business may have failed, but it doesn't mean God isn't faithful. The marriage may have been terminated, but that doesn't mean God doesn't care.

Life becomes so much simpler to see God's love when situations are not seen as ultimate failures or successes until God receives praise through them. God can only turn bad into good in our lives when we allow him the time to work long after we feel something or someone has died.

Before my wife and I had kids and we had time to spend some of our summer Saturday afternoons lounging in front of the TV, on occasion we would find ourselves watching the painter Bob Ross. If I'm being honest, after flipping through the few stations our antenna actually picked up, we were often forced to watch him due to nothing else being on.

Bob Ross's show is basically him starting with a blank canvass and then he walks his viewers through creating a beautiful painting. His red afro, quirky mannerisms, and bellbottom pants draw you in like a moth to the fire. You're not sure how it happens, but somehow you find yourself hooked on watching him paint and talk about making "happy little trees" and "joyful little mountains."

Although Bob Ross certainly seems to have enjoyed the 60's a little too much (if you know what I mean), the guy is an amazing painter. My favorite part of the show comes about three-quarters of the way in. The blank canvass is no longer blank. It holds a masterpiece of exquisite trees with sunrays glistening off shimmering lakes nestled in the foothills of grand mountains in the background. The painting seems perfect just the way it is.

Then it happens. Without fail, right when you think Bob Ross is going to tell you to tune in next week for another odd but entertaining experience of watching him paint, he gets out the thick brush, dabs it in some dark color, and generously adds it to the canvas, seemingly ruining the masterpiece that should have been.

My mouth drops, Bethany and I complain that he just ruined it, and I start getting nervous for him because the show is nearing its end. I'm always waiting for him to get flustered, breakdown in panic, and admit he just totally jacked-up his painting and will now have to start over next week. But it never happens that way.

He then goes for the little brush and calmly dabs together a mixture of whites, blues, and greens. He then adds this new mixture of color to the dark splotch I feel has ruined the whole painting. He adds some sun rays and flowers and a few bushes. After about five minutes, the dark blob of paint is no longer a dark blob of paint but rather a colorful, twisting oak tree or a beautiful log cabin or whatever Bob Ross felt like making that week. What I thought was going to be a blemish is now the finishing touch. It completes the whole work of art. Without it, I can see the painting would have been average at best. Now it is truly a masterpiece.

But what would have happened if Bob Ross wasn't allowed to finish what he started? What if he was painting, added the splotch, and then someone told him to take a hike because he just ruined the whole thing? What could have been a masterpiece is now an average painting that is ruined and tossed into the dumpster.

That's what it's like when we turn from God in the middle of him working to glorify himself in our lives. The master artist needs to be allowed to finish his work. What we feel is going to be a blemish, God wants to make as his finishing touch.

Jesus told his disciples that Lazarus's sickness would not "end" in death. But then Lazarus dies, the splotch of dark paint is generously applied, and it seems the hope of a happy ending is lost. Maybe Jesus messed up? Maybe God really doesn't love Lazarus? As the disciples wonder what is going on, Jesus says to them, ". . . for your sake I am glad I was not there, so that you may believe" (John 11:15).

Jesus then raises Lazarus from the dead, Lazarus and the sisters love him like never before, and the display of God's power causes many people to put their faith in Jesus (John 11:43). As Lazarus was coming out of the tomb in his grave clothes, I imagine Jesus turning around and looking at his speechless disciples. His eyes surely said it all, "Do you believe who I am yet?"

Storms Are Meant to Reveal Who Jesus Is

The disciples were constantly viewing life through their own personalized definitions of "good." When they were walking with Jesus and saw a blind man, they asked, "Rabbi, who sinned, this man or his parents, that he was born blind?" (John

9:2). They assumed because the man had a difficult circumstance to deal with, God must be punishing him.

Like a baseball bat to a mirror, Jesus shatters their understanding of God's love when he states, "Neither this man nor his parents sinned, but this happened so that the work of God might be displayed in his life" (John 9:3). God shows his love for us by displaying his power in our lives, not by always creating pampered life experiences. God allowed the man to be born blind so that God could use his blindness to display his glory. In love, not in hate, did God let the man be born with a disability.

When Jesus sent the disciples into the storm, he was trying to teach them this very thing. In Mark 4 we have Jesus directing the disciples into the boat, telling them to sail across the lake to the other side:

> [37] A furious squall came up, and the waves broke over the boat, so that it was nearly swamped. [38] Jesus was in the stern, sleeping on a cushion. The disciples woke him and said to him, "Teacher, don't you care if we drown?"

> [39] He got up, rebuked the wind and said to the waves, "Quiet! Be still!" Then the wind died down and it was completely calm.

> [40] He said to his disciples, "Why are you so afraid? Do you still have no faith?"

> [41] They were terrified and asked each other, "Who is this? Even the wind and the waves obey him!"

Let's get our facts straight here. Jesus is the one who sends them into the storm (verse 35), Jesus is in the boat when the squall almost sinks them (verse 37), but he waits to save the disciples until they call out to him (verse 39). It must have been confusing for them to be in a near death experience Jesus brought them into with him right in the boat by their side.

If Jesus wasn't there, perhaps the storm would have made more sense to them. "I told you, Peter," Thomas might say, "we should never have tried to cross this lake without Jesus. You know he brings us good luck." But their good luck charm was right in the boat with them. Perhaps Jesus allows the boat to almost sink to teach the disciples that just because he is with them, it doesn't mean hard times are not ahead. Jesus allows the storm for a greater purpose. He forgoes their immediate comfort and allows them to almost drown not because he doesn't love them, but because he desires to show how great and powerful his love really is.

Jesus wasn't upset that the disciples woke him up. He was upset that they were afraid. He didn't say, "Why did you disturb me? Do you know how long it's been since I've gotten some solid sleep?" All he said was, "Why are you so afraid? Do you still have no faith?" (verse 40). Clearly Jesus is upset because they doubted him. They didn't wake Jesus up saying, "Jesus, there is a storm upon us and we know you are the only one who can save us." Instead they woke him up with panic stricken faces and yelled in fear, "Teacher, don't you care if we drown?" (verse 38).

When Jesus questions their faith, I believe he is questioning their faith in his love for them as their Savior. Faith in God's power and love squashes all fear. I think Jesus was saying, "I know you don't have any idea of how much I love you or of how much power I hold, and you just proved it by doubting me. I didn't bring you into this storm because I don't love you. I brought you into this storm to show the power of my love for you." Jesus knew the disciples would never ask the question, "Who is this? Even the wind and the waves obey him!" (verse 41) if they didn't witness the power of Jesus in the middle of a storm.

Rather than spare them the immediate danger of almost drowning, he lets them endure the fear of death so that they might begin to understand that Jesus alone brings life. It was good for the disciples to almost drown because they learned Jesus has the power to save and is worthy of all adoration. Perhaps the point of the storm was not only to test the disciples' faith, it was to prove and display the faithfulness of God.

Since the disciples didn't get it this first time, in Matthew 14 Jesus sends them into another storm, but this time he is not with them. Seeing them struggle, he allows the storm to get really bad, and then he goes out to them by walking on the water. The disciples doubt it's Jesus, so Peter asks to walk on the water to Jesus to prove if it's really him. Jesus tells Peter to come, Peter walks on the water, doubts and begins to sink, but then Jesus rescues him. Once Jesus and Peter step into the boat it states, ". . . the wind died down. Then those who were in the boat worshiped him, saying, 'Truly you are the Son of God'" (Matthew 14:32-33).

In both storms, Jesus had to let the disciples get completely terrified before they would call out to him. But as soon as they gave Jesus the opportunity to glorify himself in their trouble, Jesus stopped the storm and gave them great peace and joy. The point of the storms in our lives is always the same. God wants to glorify himself by revealing Jesus is the great Savior. He wants us to first call into question, "Who is this? Even the wind and the waves obey him!" (Mark 4:41). And then he wants us to answer, "Truly you are the Son of God" (Matthew 14:32).

Often times the faster we call out and allow God the opportunity to be praised, the faster he stops the storm. Maybe God will remove you from that job you despise when you start worshipping him in it. Maybe he will begin to grow your church when you honor God with the few people he has given you. Maybe the marriage will improve when you give God your whole heart even in its dysfunction. God isn't mean, he just knows the best thing for us is to learn to glorify him.

It's not as though Jesus is compassionless for us in our difficulties. Jesus wept over the death of Lazarus (John 11:35) and Jesus immediately stopped the storm as soon as the disciples asked him to (Mark 4:39). But Jesus, in love, is always willing to allow short-term discomfort if his splendor can shine and produce eternal transformation and joy. Jesus knows if we want to walk on water, we need storms to call out to him during.

8

Power Over Our Past

Pain insists upon being attended to. God whispers to us in our pleasures, speaks in our consciences, but shouts in our pains. It is his megaphone to rouse a deaf world. - C.S. Lewis[1]

But the pot he was shaping from the clay was marred in his hands; so the potter formed it into another pot, shaping it as seemed best to him. -Jeremiah 18:4-6

One evening my dad and stepmom stopped over for a visit, wanting to see the grandkids. As my stepmom and wife were holding the baby, "ooing and ahhing" over the slightest changes in facial expressions, my dad and I wandered into my backyard for a quick escape.

With a limp due to the stroke, my dad slowly trailed behind me as I made my way to the garage. As we sat on my workout equipment, chatting about more manly things than how cute the baby's "goo goo gagas" were, my dad saw a verse I had posted on the wall, Isaiah 57:15. Slowly, he read it aloud, "For this is what the high and exalted One says— he who lives forever, whose name is holy: 'I live in a high and holy place, but also with the one who is contrite and lowly in spirit, to revive the spirit of the lowly and to revive the heart of the contrite.'"

Scratching his chin slowly as he so often does, still looking at the verse, he replied, "Isaiah is a good book." Smiling a bit and adding a slow head shake to his chin scratching, he whispered, "This is what the Sovereign LORD, the Holy One of Israel, says: 'In repentance and rest is your salvation, in quietness and trust is your strength."

"Where's that verse from?" I asked.

He let out a little laugh, "I don't remember. Somewhere in Isaiah, though." Another short pause, the kind he likes to give just before a story of his begins, and then it happens. He starts laughing and shaking his head faster, "Oh, boy! He sure did humble me that morning of the great flood . . . ."Ah, yes, The Great Flood story. I had heard it so many times before I can recite the details better than him.

Before I was ever born, my dad was a fitness fanatic. His desire for competition and his love for exercise found perfect expression in the sport of cycling. He would spend countless hours riding his bike. Eighty-mile rides after a full day of work at the construction site was standard for him. In the 1980's he even tried out for the Olympics. He didn't make it, but he was good enough to qualify to try. As that story goes, he ended up beating some of the top riders in the country because a horrible storm caused much of the racers to drop out. My dad was a lot of things back then, but a quitter wasn't on the list.

People who never give up, like my dad, have a lot of things going for them. But their tenacity can also be a curse, requiring God to have to work a little harder to get their attention (For better or worse, I've inherited this trait as well).

After his stroke my dad found solace back on the saddle of his bike. He couldn't walk well. He couldn't pick up simple things like a cup with his left hand. He couldn't think as clearly as he once did. Basically, he couldn't do anything as good as he used to, but what he could still do was ride his bike. So that's what he did. He will tell you now, however, cycling was taking over too much. Marriage and other parts of his life were suffering. God needed to get his attention again.

As he was riding one early morning as he always did, a serious storm began to develop. Instead of turning back, by dad pressed on just as he had done so many times before, not wanting to miss out on any training. It was so early in the morning it was still dark outside. When he came to a valley, way out in the country where no one was around, he saw the road was flooded. He pressed ahead.

As he rode through the flooded street in the valley, the water began to rise higher and higher, eventually becoming chest deep. He unclipped from his pedals and tried to carry his bike through it. But because of the current, the bike shoes he was wearing, and his severe limp due to the stroke, he began to lose traction with the ground. The water was starting to overtake him.

He suddenly realized more was at stake than his training ride. Clenching his state of the art bike with his good hand, unwilling to lose it in the flood, he struggled to keep his head above water as he flapped his bad arm like a wounded duck sinking quickly. Finally, he began to reach the other side. But the struggle was not without cost. As he got on his bike and road home, he realized something was wrong with his right leg, which was his good one.

A trip to the doctor discovered a micro fracture. Unable to ride and after recounting his near death experience over his desire to train at all cost, God began to work in him. Because of his over dependence on riding, he was on the verge of losing it all. As he blew off the dust from his Bible and cracked it open, he came to Isaiah 30:15, "This is what the Sovereign LORD, the

Holy One of Israel, says: In repentance and rest is your salvation, in quietness and trust is your strength . . . ."

Humbled, my dad finally gave his life back over to God in ways that he had been resisting for years. In kindness, God had to allow his sinful determination to come face to face with The Great Flood. I can relate to my dad's story because it has been my story over and over again as well. In some form or another, it's all of our stories. We run, God allows us to, hopefully we are humbled, and when we return to him he always redeems. I don't think God enjoys allowing our sin to get so bad it nearly kills us, but it seems he loves his children too much to spare us of this pain.

A Desire for Death Can Wake Us Up

In the last chapter we discovered God uses trials in our lives so he can glorify himself through them. But what about temptations? The Bible makes clear God can cause a trial but he will never cause a temptation (James 1:13, Hebrews 6:18). For God to tempt someone to sin would go against his holy and loving nature. He knows a trial can be a loving thing for his children because it can draw them closer to him (James 1:2-4, Romans 5:3-5). Sin, however, always has the opposite effect, so he never tempts us (Psalm 66:18). He uses temptation, but he never initiates it.

Yet if we were to sit over a cup of coffee and discuss our pasts, our sinful wanderings would surely take up much of our stories. If sin separates us from God, why does he allow us to do it? If our purpose in life is to glorify God, have we ruined or missed our purpose due to our sinful pasts? By our reactions after we sin, it seems that many of us would answer, "Yes, we have blown our purpose when we turn from God in sin."

I have noticed two reactions to sin when a deep repentance is not present: denial and suicide. The first is pretty obvious. Rather than face the shame and humiliation of admitting that one is a sinner, they simply deny it. Most people are willing to admit they have sinned but they don't like admitting that at the core of who they are, they are a sinner. We do this because we doubt there is a real cure to such a huge problem. We can overlook a mistake, a sin here and there, but how can one handle the shocking realization of being wicked at heart? Denial is often the sad solution for most.

If, however, people are more honest about themselves or have committed a sin so bad they are unable to deny their own sinfulness, if they do not seek Christ's grace, they feel the only release from their shame is death. They commit suicide, either physically or metaphorically through depression in heart and mind caused by the guilt of their own undeniable sinfulness.

Growing up, my dad and I would often go over the Richardson's house. My dad was friends with Mr. Richardson because they were both bike riders. Since I played hockey with the oldest son, it just made sense for us all to be friends. As the son and I took turns taking pucks to the shins in the backyard as we rotated who played goalie, our dad's would hangout and visit in the house, talking about the upcoming races and how their training had been going. Mrs. Richardson would often offer us deserts or lemonade as the other siblings would be milling about as kids do. By all accounts they seemed like a happy little family.

Then one day my dad told me we couldn't go over there anymore. When I asked why not, he began to share the details he probably should have hid from a young boy. Mr. Richardson had finally been caught in adultery. Apparently he had been unfaithful for years towards his wife, but he kept denying there was any big problem with what he was doing.

When his wife discovered his infidelity and Mr. Richardson had to finally come to terms with his massive mistakes, instead of opening his Bible like my dad did, he felt he had ruined his life so badly there was no point finishing it out. Just like Judas who hanged himself once he finally realized how evil his actions were towards Christ (Matthew 27:1-10), Mr. Richardson could no longer deny his sinful past. Hopeless because of his guilt, he took out his gun and killed himself.

People kill themselves, both physically and metaphorically, because they doubt God's grace is greater than their guilt. We know intrinsically we were made to worship and please God, and when we fail in this we often run rather than repent because we feel there is no cure to our failure. People often feel they have blown God's will for their lives when they sin in huge ways; since they can no longer deny their sinfulness, they cannot live long under its shame. But God is always hoping our desire for death will lead us to wakeup and repent.

He Lets Us Go to the Distant Country Rather Than Die Just Out of Reach

Aside from denial or suicide, there is only one other option: turning back to God, for as my dad realized, "In repentance and rest is your salvation" (Isaiah 30:15). God allows us to be tempted and even allows us to sin because he is confident in his ability to turn anything for his glory through his grace.

He allows temptations from the spiritual forces of evil in the heavenly realms (Ephesians 6:12), from the world (1 John 2:16), and from our flesh (Romans 7:20) to awaken us from our dullness over our desperate need for Jesus (1 Corinthians 5:5). Even when we are Christians, God allows sin to get progressively worse in our lives if we are not repenting because he wants our true selves in Christ to be repulsed by our sinfulness and wakeup so we turn back to God.

If you do not see the harm in getting drunk, God will allow you to get a DUI. If you don't see the harm in gossip, he will allow you to ruin your relationships with your best friends by betraying their trust. If you don't see the harm in lust, he will allow you to go down that next dark road of perversion until finally you come to your senses and realize, "Wait, I do not want these things."

That is why so many testimonies include details of having to "hit rock bottom." Sometimes it takes a great darkness to enter our lives before we realize we actually hate all shades of grey. From God's perspective, an unrepentant heart over "smaller sins" is still an unrepentant heart. What's the difference if someone's relationship with God is hindered because of smoking cigarettes compared to someone addicted to heroin who is involved in prostitution in order to pay for the drugs? Certainly there are greater natural consequences to some sins, but all sins can separate people from God if allowed to take God's place in the heart, even though some sins seem less sinful.

C.S. Lewis states, "Prostitutes are in no danger of finding their present life so satisfactory that they cannot turn to God: the proud, the avaricious, the self-righteous, are in that danger."[2] God allows us to run from him in pride so our sin grows worse because he would rather have us broken and humbled than not at all.

In Luke 15:11-31, we have one of Jesus' most famous parables. I'll summarize it here, but if you haven't read it in awhile, I encourage you to do so now. There is a rich father with two sons. The older son stays with his father and works hard to earn his dad's love. The younger son, however, asks the father to give him his inheritance early so he can go party and have a good time away from the father in a distant country. The father gives him the money, the son runs away, but then he hits rock bottom one day due to a famine. He squandered his wealth with prostitutes and wild living and now is forced to work on a pig farm.

Then he repents towards his father, his father forgives him, and then the father throws a huge party to celebrate the return of his son who he thought was dead. The older son gets frustrated that his father is celebrating the return of the sinful son because the older son has been steadily working but never received a party. The father responds, "You are always with me, and everything I have is yours. But we had to celebrate and be glad, because this brother of yours was dead and is alive again; he was lost and is found" (Luke 15:31-32).

What's crazy about all this is that the father gives the younger son the early inheritance. Sometimes the scariest thing is when God gives us what we want. God loves us so much he will allow us to have what will make us miserable so we will finally accept that only he can make us satisfied. What if the father didn't let the son have the money and the son never left? The son would have just lived at home, thinking he would be better off without his dad's love. He would never have gone down the roads that woke him up to the reality of his father's goodness. The son's rebellion was not the father's first option, but in the end the father used it to show the son his love.

Years ago I remember hearing the testimony of a young woman who was about to get baptized. As she sat on the stage explaining all the horrible things she did before giving her life to Christ, she veered from her written testimony and questioned why God didn't make her repentant before she sinned in these terrible ways that had obviously wounded her so deeply. She was grateful for his forgiveness but could not understand why in his sovereignty he didn't stop her from her shameful past. If he has the power to do anything, she reasoned, why didn't he stop her from sinning and hurting herself and others?

So why doesn't God stop us before we make huge, hurtful mistakes in our lives? Because he knows without them some of us will never really return home. "Then call on me when you are in trouble, and I will rescue you, and you will give me glory" (Psalm 50:15 NLT).

He allows our sins to get progressively worse because he would rather us go to the distant evil country but return home rather than die one town away from his embrace. Whether one mile or one hundred miles away, God is not satisfied until we are truly back in his arms. Like the father in the parable, he lets us leave in hopes he will see us one day way off in the distance, returning home so he can run to us while we are still a long way off, and so he can throw a party once we get to where he always knew was the best place for us – right next to him.

Like a good doctor willing to cause a person immense pain in chemo therapy because he knows the treatment could save the person's life, God allows painful mistakes to happen in hopes they will result in repentance (Psalm 83:16). A good doctor is willing to amputate if he knows the painful removal of a limb will stop the spread of disease (Matthew 5:29-30). Doctors overlook pain in treatment because the person's life, not comfort, is their primary concern.

Jesus came for the sick, not the healthy. Everyone is sick (Romans 3:23), but not everyone knows it. God allows us to do whatever we must for us to realize how sick we are. He certainly gives us warning after warning so we can avoid sin, but he is also willing to allow us to hurt ourselves greatly because he knows he is skilled enough to heal us deeply through the pain.

The Work of Christ Is Always Enough

The father in Jesus' parable wanted to show his love to both sons. The obedient son was loved by the father through an ongoing relationship with him, even though the older son didn't value this (Luke 15:31). Since the younger son was disobedient, the father showed his love the only way left for him to do it – by forgiving him.

The whole point of the parable is to show the great love of the Father. Jesus is trying to highlight God's love. God will show the world his love by blessing peoples' obedience with a deep relationship with himself. However, he will also show his love through peoples' disobedience by totally forgiving them when they repent.

The point of the story is not to highlight the actions of humans. People are never the ultimate point. We may benefit, but God's glory is always the point of every story. You can't ruin God's ultimate purpose for your life when you sin and repent because God's purpose is for him to magnify himself through you. And he can do that through your obedience or through your repentance after your disobedience.

God cares about us so much that in order to get us to turn and truly seek him, he is willing to allow us to make massive mistakes at great cost to ourselves and his Son. If we won't glorify God through benefitting from obedience to him by walking in his Spirit, he will glorify himself by making us examples of his kindness.

> But God is so rich in mercy, and he loved us so much, that even though we were dead because of our sins, he gave us life when he raised Christ from the dead. (It is only by God's grace that you have been saved!) For he raised us from the dead along with Christ and seated us with him in the heavenly realms because we are united with Christ Jesus. *So God can point to us in all future ages as examples of the incredible wealth of his grace and kindness toward us, as shown in all he has done for us who are united with Christ Jesus.* (Ephesians 2:4-7 NLT)

My sinful past is solved when I live for nothing but God because only God can turn my sinful past into something glorious. By the world's standards, a failure will forever be a failure. But God can turn sin into something useful to himself by displaying his power to redeem through Christ who overrules our failures. Our sinful history can be his redemption story if we repent and allow him to glorify himself. God's love, authority, and all of his beauty is never seen as clearly than when he displays his great kindness and grace to the undeserving through the gospel.

When he reverses the intentions of Satan by forgiving and redeeming us, it shows his complete sovereignty and power over evil, bringing himself praise and honor from those he saves from the devil's clutches. What was meant for evil, only God has the power to turn for good (Genesis 50:20).

It's a great relief when you realize you are not at the center of the story and that God is. He's the hero of the story. He's the one everything depends on. If my purpose in life is to please God, when I sin, I have not missed my ultimate purpose. I have only truly and totally missed my purpose if I sin and don't repent, because God pleases himself through redeeming us, and this is dependent upon him.

He can work out everything, even our sins, for his purpose when we turn to him (Romans 8:28). So whether through joy stemming from obedience to God or joy stemming from underserved kindness, Jesus can always fulfill his original plan for our lives, which is to bring glory to himself, when we turn and worship him after receiving his amazing grace.

The obedient will have fewer natural consequences to deal with due to sin, but you can't ruin God's ultimate plan for your life if you repent. This is not an excuse to disobey; for if we continue in our sin it is evidence our salvation is not genuine (1 John 3:6, Romans 6:1, 2). Rather, his never ending fountain of grace is the means God uses to turn the worst of sinners into the ones who love him most. For those who have been forgiven much, love much (Luke 7:47).

I wish I could have talked to that girl giving her testimony who wondered why God didn't stop her from her painful past. I would have told her he didn't stop her because he didn't have to. The power of Jesus to save, given to us through his death and resurrection when we believe in him through faith, is more than enough to overrule our every sin.

We expected God to show his love by stopping our sin. But as I've heard many pastors put it, if God always meets our expectations, he will never have the chance to exceed them. When Jesus is involved, the scenes of our greatest failures can turn into the scenes of God's greatest miracles in our lives. So when we are reminded of our past rebellion, this should no longer bring shame but praise to God for having the power to redeem us from that rebellion.

By stating we wish God would have stopped us form making those mistakes that still haunt us, we are confessing we don't believe what Jesus did is enough to truly turn our sinful pasts for his glory. When we wish such things, we are proving that we doubt his faithfulness is greater than our failures. But when we receive his grace, we gain the power over our painful pasts. God doesn't need to micromanage our lives. What Jesus did truly is enough to turn blemishes into beauty, to turn what was meant for evil into good. God didn't need to stop you from your sins to bring himself glory.

He sent Christ instead.

9

Salvation Exalts the Savior

For the sake of your name, LORD, forgive my iniquity, though it is great. -Psalm 25:11

God chose the lowly things of this world and the despised things—and the things that are not—to nullify the things that are, so that no one may boast before him. It is because of him that you are in Christ Jesus, who has become for us wisdom from God—that is, our righteousness, holiness and redemption. Therefore, as it is written: "Let the one who boasts boast in the Lord." -1 Corinthians 1:28-31

The Medal of Honor is the highest military award in all the US Armed Forces. It is only given to those soldiers who have displayed the utmost gallantry and intrepidity at the risk of his or her life above and beyond the call of duty.

One such recipient was Master Sergeant Roy P. Benavidez for his heroics in the Vietnam War. On the morning of May 2, 1968, a 12-man Special Forces Reconnaissance Team was inserted by helicopters into a dense jungle area west of Loc Ninh, Vietnam. Their mission was to gather intelligence information in an area heavily patrolled by the North Vietnam Army (NVA).

The highly trained team began taking heavy fire, became pinned down, and called for an extraction. The only way out was by helicopter, and after three attempts by pilots, the plight of these 12 men seemed more hopeless by the minute.

Meanwhile, Benavidez was back at the base helping coordinate extraction attempts by radio. Realizing the men were either dead or wounded and thus unable to run to the pickup zone, he jumped into the helicopter in order to help. Benavidez ran over 200 feet from the helicopter to the pinned down men. Because of the NVA's heavy assaults, before he even reached the men he was shot in the leg and wounded in the face and head from an exploding grenade.

Despite his injuries, when he arrived to the surviving 8 men out of the original 12, he took charge. He ordered them to make defensive positions and directed gun fire to create a landing zone. After throwing a smoke canister to guide the pilot in, he dragged half of the team to the chopper and then ran alongside it to provide protective fire as it moved to pick up the remaining survivors.

Benavidez then ran to get the classified documents left behind. As he was doing this, he was shot in the abdomen and wounded in the back from more grenade shrapnel. To make matters worse, at nearly the same time he was hit, the pilot was mortally wounded, crashing the helicopter. Benavidez gathered himself once more, got the wounded out of the wreckage, made defensive positions again, and directed fire with the quickly diminishing ammo supply.

He began to run from man to man, giving them water and instilling in them the will to fight and survive. They called in the coordinates for the nearby gunships to provide heavy artillery fire. As he was administering first aid, he was shot again in the thigh. But as another helicopter arrived, Benavidez once more loaded in the wounded. He then went for one more sweep of the area to make sure all classified documents were collected and to see if he could retrieve anymore of the bodies of those who had been killed. But on his way, he was clubbed in the head by an enemy soldier, breaking his jaw. Hand to hand combat ensued. Benavidez took out his knife and killed the enemy. Only then did he jump into the helicopter, barely surviving the 37 wounds that had been inflicted upon him from the NVA.[1]

Because of his voluntary heroics, at least eight men were saved and he thus earned the highest praise any US Armed Forces' member could ever receive. On February 24, 1981, President Ronald Reagan presented Benavidez with the Medal of Honor. Turning to the press, the President stated, "If the story of his heroism were a movie script, you would not believe it."[2]

But what if at the ceremony, instead of giving the medal to this hero who earned it, the President made Benavidez pin medals on the men he saved? What if after making him pin the medals on, the President then asked Benavidez to praise these men by pointing out in each of them the qualities they possessed that made him want to save them?

Of course this would be utterly ridiculous! Those men didn't get saved because they were more special than others. They got saved because Benavidez was special. Therefore, only he got the medal. Benavidez received his honor, but when we make our salvation all about us, we rob Jesus of his. Great acts of courage benefit the helpless, but they are supposed to glorify the heroic.

Me-Centeredness Hurts Me Most

One of the greatest hindrances to living a God-centered life is our modern evangelistic efforts. We try to convert people by telling them how special God thinks they are. But God doesn't save people because we are so special. He saves people to show how special he is. We are benefitted the most, but we are benefitted so we might worship him. Salvation was never meant to make much of humans. Salvation exalts the Savior. And the sooner we embrace this the sooner our power and joy will grow.

If you are going to set out on a journey over an eternal time span, one degree off from the correct coordinates makes all the difference. You won't end up one degree away from where you wanted to go. As you travel further and further on the wrong straight line, the line you are on will veer farther and farther from the line you should be on until you are an infinite amount of miles away. Likewise, anyone who has built a structure of any kind knows the foundation is everything. Even as a little child builds a tower with blocks, the higher the tower gets, the more the foundation is tested. When we don't spend the time starting right, things come crashing down around us really quick.

At the start of most of our conversions, we were told that Jesus died for us. Obviously this is true. Jesus died to take away my sins because I was powerless to do that for myself. So in that sense Jesus did die for us. But what was his ultimate motivation in saving the world? It was his same motivation he had for everything he ever did – to glorify the Father.

In a greater sense, therefore, Jesus didn't die for humans. Jesus died for the Father. I don't mean he died to save the Father. Certainly Jesus' death saves us, but it was done out of a desire to please the Father. It was to make much of God by showing forever the incredible wealth of his kindness (Ephesians 2:7). If it didn't please God to save us, Jesus wouldn't have done it. Thankfully it did please God to save us, so that's what Jesus did!

But it wasn't as though Jesus wanted to die on the cross like some lover of pain. What he wanted was to glorify his Father by saving us. "Now my soul is troubled, and what shall I say? 'Father, save me from this hour'? No, it was for this very reason I came to this hour. Father, glorify your name!" (John 12:27-28).

Of course Jesus loved the people he came to serve, but he served them as a way of honoring God, which includes himself. When he was giving his disciples a lesson on how to become great, he said, ". . . whoever wants to become great among you must be your servant, and whoever wants to be first must be your slave— just as the Son of Man did not come to be served, but to serve, and to give his life as a ransom for many" (Matthew 10:26-28). Jesus came "to serve," but his service is in the context of "whoever wants to become great among you must be your servant." Jesus came to give his life as a ransom for many, but he gave his life as a ransom for many to show his greatness.

If his ultimate motivation was simply to serve people regardless of God's praise, he would not only be serving people, he would be worshipping them. When we subtract the motive behind God's grace, we put ourselves at the center of the universe, making ourselves miserable creatures in the process because we are separating ourselves from God's true intentions for us. We must reset our foundation so we can live out our true purpose as Jesus did, the purpose of pleasing the Father.

Satan loves when preachers get on stage to tell people how special they are, so special Jesus died just for them. What a lie he has given us! If Jesus died because we are special apart from him, why did he need to die at all? To say he saved us because he saw potential in us is like saying we earned our spot on his team, that we somehow deserved to be saved. This type of thinking robs God of the praise only he deserves and takes away the pleasure we get when we give it to him (2 Corinthians 5:15, Philippians 3:7-10).

Additionally, when we start the Christian journey thinking God saved us because of our greatness, our sense of entitlement only grows rather than dies. Jesus said the more we die to our selfishness the more alive we will become to him. How contradictory would Christianity be if on one hand we were told that we deserve God's grace and on the other hand grace, by it's very definition, is an undeserved gift?

It's so important to start this journey knowing God saved us for his glory because for the rest of our lives God will be giving us tasks meant for his glory, not our comforts. People feel betrayed by God when he gives them hard tasks and difficult life circumstances because they thought Christianity was all about their salvation and selfish pleasure, not God's glory. And why wouldn't they think this if we tell them from the start how special they are? We are all loved by God, but we are not deserving of his love. There's a big difference.

Jesus died because he wanted to make us special to show his great love, not because we already were special. We were God's enemies before Jesus saved us (Romans 5:8), objects of wrath that God freely gave mercy to so that no one can boast except in him (Ephesians 2:4-9, 1 Corinthians 1:28-31). Jesus is exalted above all else and has the name above all names not because he died on the cross for people, but because he died on the cross for people "to the glory of God the Father" (Philippians 2:6-11). The lyrics of a song in heaven reveal why Jesus is worthy of all praise:

> "You are worthy to take the scroll and to open
> its seals, because you were slain, and with your
> blood you purchased for God persons from
> every tribe and language and people and nation.
> You have made them to be a kingdom and
> priests to serve our God, and they will reign on
> the earth" (Revelations 5:9-10).

Jesus didn't die to purchase men; he died to purchase men "for God." He didn't make believers a kingdom of priests; he made us a kingdom of priests "to serve our God." If you subtract the motive you subtract the whole link that explains why everything exists. We exist for God's pleasure and thus function with the most joy when we embrace this reality.

Viewing Jesus' mission as helping us live our best life now without any thought to his desire for us to worship God in service to him is not only cheating yourself of immense joy, it is also downright dangerous. When we view people at the center of God's saving work rather than his desire to express his brilliance, our coordinates are changed and we are no longer on the straight path to worshipping him forever but rather on a path leading to worshipping ourselves more and more. Self-worship is the very thing that kept Satan from heaven (Ezekiel 28:16-17, Isaiah 14:12-15). If it worked on him, Satan knows this temptation can work on us.

Heaven and Hell Validate that God-Centeredness Is Biblical

If you don't have tears in your eyes and a deep grief in your heart when you talk about hell, you can't possibly comprehend even the smallest percent of its horror. But as horrible as hell is to our human minds, we cannot deny its reality.

I hate the idea of people going to hell for eternity, but as Augustine said, "If you believe what you like in the Gospel, and reject what you don't like, it is not the Gospel you believe, but yourself." The Bible clearly states that heaven and hell are both real and eternal (Deuteronomy 32:22, Psalm 9:17, Matthew 10:28, John 3:16, 14:2, Revelation 20:10, 15) therefore if I choose to believe in heaven I must also believe in hell, no matter how disturbing it may be to me.

Why would a God of love create the reality of hell? The answer is pretty simple: A God who was *only* love wouldn't. Without pitting God's qualities against each other or denying his fully perfect, loving nature, we must also realize that God is more than just love. In actuality, if you wanted to pick out one quality of God that most clearly defines him, it wouldn't be his love. It would actually be his holiness.

When Isaiah saw the Lord seated on his throne, high and exalted, the seraphs were not praising God with, "Loving, loving, loving, is the Lord Almighty." What they were calling out was "Holy, holy, holy is the Lord Almighty; the whole earth is full of his glory" (Isaiah 6:3). His perfect holiness is what allows his love. If he was not perfectly holy and could embrace sin, then he would also be unable to love as fully as he does because his perfect nature would be compromised. So in reply to the common question of "How can a loving God send people to hell?" the answer is found in the counter question, "How can a holy God not send unredeemed sinners to hell?"

Hell is the proof that all existence is not about humans. It's about God. If God was more concerned with saving humans than with the display of his holiness, hell would only be for the demons. You should run from any church or pastor who refuses to talk about the reality of hell. Anyone who avoids this topic fractions the Bible to make it about something it's not – you.

The Bible is not primarily about us. It is primarily *for* us because we are the ones who need it, but it's *about* God and his glorification through his actions to save the lost. People who want to make Christianity centered on people rather than Christ's magnification are hazardous to be around. What they say is often not totally wrong, but it is not totally right either.

When they say that God loves you, he'll save you, and he'll help you live a better life, they are not in error. They are at fault when this is all that they say. Even if it is unintentional, they subtly steer you away from the whole truth. The full truth is that God saves people who receive his grace and destroys people who don't because people are not the main point (Jeremiah 12:14-17). If the truth is that God is for God first, which benefits us, then hell must also be true. If God is for people first, then hell would make no sense. You know what kind of theology you have by your view of hell. A me-centered worldview translates into no hell. But a God-centered worldview must have a hell. Since hell is clearly a biblical reality, so must be God's desire for people to love him above all else.

But how does hell glorify God if he is most glorified through our good? Let's set the record straight: God doesn't enjoy sending people to hell, ". . . he is patient with you, not wanting anyone to perish, but everyone to come to repentance" (2 Peter 3:9). He sent Jesus to rescue us from it because salvation rather than damnation pleases him more. Ezekiel 18:32 states, "For I take no pleasure in the death of anyone, declares the Sovereign Lord. Repent and live!"

But since God's exaltation is his highest priority (if it wasn't he would no longer be God), he will still glorify himself through people who refuse his grace. To allow them into heaven without the blood of Jesus would compromise his divine nature and ruin heaven for everyone, so he can't do this because it would contradict his love and holiness. The only way he can express his worth through unrepentant people is through giving them what they ask for – the absence of himself.

Hell is so awful because God is totally absent there (or as some theologians explain the only quality of God there is his wrath). Heaven is so amazing because our union with God will be perfect. Hell magnifies the greatness of God through his absence by showing how wretched an existence is without his grace. Heaven magnifies the greatness of God through complete joy caused by his presence and pure grace. If people refuse to love God by experiencing the fullness of his joy in heaven, he will display his greatness by allowing them to experience the complete lack of his joy in hell. "The Lord works out everything for his own ends, even the wicked for a day of disaster" (Proverbs 16:4).

To put it simply, I always have a greater appreciation for all the work my wife does around the house after she has been away for a period of time. Her value to the family is seen even when she's not there because the absence of all the good she brings is so obviously missing. Where God's grace is absent he is still glorified by the glaring void of goodness for which only he deserves credit.

Earth stands between heaven and hell. What many people refuse to understand is that every good gift on earth is because of God and everything evil is because of God's broken relationship with the world caused by sin (Psalm 145:9,15-20, Acts 14:17, James 1:16-17). Our time on earth is our time to choose what part of earth we want to experience forever.

When people enjoy the pleasures of earth and yet reject Jesus, they are enjoying God's gifts and yet choosing against the Giver. Thus, when their time is over on earth, they find themselves in hell without any of earth's pleasures because unlike earth there is zero percent of God's grace there (2 Thessalonians 1:8-9). When people accept God's grace, they find themselves in heaven to enjoy the full measure of the pure pleasures they experienced on earth because unlike earth, heaven is one-hundred percent absent of the sin that hinders our fellowship with God.

Besides, to let someone into heaven when they are still a God-hater, still a non-worshipper, would be hell itself. In heaven we will be filled with joy because we will be able to worship God perfectly. Heaven's focus will be God and our worship of him. Therefore, if someone self-absorbed went there, they would despise it.

Was this not the very reason Satan sabotaged himself? Surely he knew he would lose in a battle against God. Yet because of his self-worship he could no longer stand worshipping God and figured being thrown out was no worse than his current loathing. He freely chose hell because he was already there as he hated his existence in heaven because it revolved around the Lord and not himself. People, just like Satan, choose hell by pursuing self-worship and God's absence in their life. Loving God is our heaven. Not loving God becomes our hell.

Jeremiah 2:35 (NLT) states, "And yet you say, 'I have done nothing wrong. Surely God isn't angry with me!' But now I will punish you severely because you claim you have not sinned." We are sent to hell because we sinned, but we don't go to heaven because we don't sin. We go to heaven because we admit our sin, receive God's grace expressed in Christ, and repent of our sin to follow Jesus. When we refuse his grace we rob him of his chance to show his greatness the way he most desires. People who go to heaven or hell are both sinners apart from Jesus. The only difference is that one group of people allowed God to express his splendor through his grace and the other didn't. Jeremiah 13:16 adds, "Give glory to the Lord your God before he brings darkness, before your feet stumble on the darkening hills." God saves us for his glory:

> "I, even I, am he who blots out your transgressions, for my own sake, and remembers your sins no more." (Isaiah 43:25)

> " . . . while we wait for the blessed hope—the appearing of the glory of our great God and Savior, Jesus Christ, who gave himself for us to redeem us from all wickedness and to purify for himself a people that are his very own, eager to do what is good." (Titus 2:13-14)

Clearly God seeks to glorify himself through offering us grace. Since salvation is meant to exalt the Savior, is it any wonder Christianity claims that there is only one path to salvation (John 14:6)? No one can come to the Father except through Jesus because God would never allow anyone but himself the praise for this marvelous act.

Notice how all other religions are based upon works because they were made by man and thus cater to the pride of people. Religion seeks prideful praise for people by giving them the chance at saving themselves through good deeds. They take the focus away from what God must do on behalf of the human and steal his praise by explaining what they believe man must do on behalf of God.

Prideful people try and get close to God by not sinning. Humble people get close to God through receiving the grace of the gospel and the result is freedom from sinning. You don't get close to God by doing good, but when you get close to him through grace he causes you to do good. This is what grace does. If we could become righteous apart from grace, we would deserve honor. Only God deserves this credit because only he has the ability to purchase a people for himself (1 Chronicles 17:21-22).

Religion is rooted in pride and self-effort while a relationship of grace is rooted in humility and absolute surrender to the will of God. Religion is so appealing to people because it is a way for them to get what they want from God but by avoiding the need to rely on him. Religion gives people the glory because what they "accomplish" is based upon what they do rather than on what they receive. As Oswald Chambers said in his classic devotional, *My Utmost for His Highest*:

> "There is a certain pride in man that will give and give, but to come and accept is another thing. I will give my life to martyrdom, I will give myself in consecration, I will do anything, but do not humiliate me to the level of the most hell-deserving sinner and tell me that all I have to do is to accept the gift of salvation through Jesus Christ.

> We have to realize that we cannot earn or win anything from God; we must either receive it as a gift or do without it. The greatest blessing spiritually is the knowledge that we are destitute; until we get there Our Lord is

powerless. He can do nothing for us if we think we are sufficient of ourselves. We have to enter into His Kingdom through the door of destitution."[3]

Pride is what causes our greatest problems because it exalts us above God. Humility is how we honor the Lord and find immense, everlasting joy in him because it places the focus on where it should be – on God's grace and glory. If you want God's favor, you need to be all about God's fame through humbly relying on his grace.

God Blesses the Humble Because the Humble Honor Him

The main message of the story of the prodigal son becomes much easier to understand when you know who the character's represent. In the beginning of Luke 15, we learn Jesus is talking to prideful Pharisees who are constantly trying to earn their salvation through fulfilling the letter of the law. We also learn he is talking to blatant sinners who have long since given up on earning their own righteousness and are thus very receptive to the grace of Jesus, unlike the Pharisees. It's pretty clear the prodigal son represents the repentant sinners, the older son represents the prideful Pharisees, and the loving father represents Jesus.

The older brother, like the Pharisees, wanted to earn what he got from his father. So the older brother got angry with the father when he freely threw a party for the sinful son, just like the Pharisees got mad when Jesus freely forgave and healed sinners (Matthew 20:1-16, Mark 2:5-12). The older son never received a party because he failed to realize the father's love could not be earned. The father was free to celebrate the prodigal son because this son was now in a place to realize he didn't deserve it.

There was no temptation for the prodigal son to take credit for the celebration. Everyone who was at that party was surely talking about the lavish love of the father on behalf of the undeserving son. The party benefitted the son but it showed the greatness of the father. If the father would have thrown a party for the older son, however, the older son and everyone present would be thinking about how praiseworthy the older son must be for the father to throw him such a party.

It's as if throughout the whole parable Jesus is saying to the Pharisees and sinners, "I welcome those who know they need me because I am the point. You and your self-effort were never supposed to be the focus. I love you because I am love. I'm going to die for you because that's the kind of God I am. I want you back in my arms not because your speech of repentance is going to be perfect or because you obeyed some of my laws, but because I am full of compassion and love. Your works can never make up for how you have turned against me. Only I am great enough to handle your sin, so only I deserve the praise and honor. I love you. Now glorify me that your joy may be complete!"

The Pharisees don't listen, however, and go on in their misery. They have no real joy because they are so self-centered, just like the older son. When the older son came home, saw the party for the sinful son, and started complaining (Luke 15:28-30), I doubt this was the first time his father heard these types of complaints. He was simply manifesting the self-centeredness that was always present in him. He was probably always giving his dad a mouthful of negativity because he always felt like he deserved more than he was getting.

People who think they deserve something from God are always the ones who end up despising him most. When people view God like Santa, they become angry at him when they don't get what they ask for even though they tried to be really good all year to get on the "nice list." But when people realize everything good humans have is given to them by grace because everyone is like the prodigal son (Romans 3:23), they are filled with a deep gratitude and joy for God who gives what no one deserves (Luke 7:47). This is why we spent the first part of this chapter talking about the importance of realizing why God really saved us. When we embrace grace and know we were undeserving, we get more joy than we ever could by lying to ourselves that we deserve anything good from God.

Because the elder son desires all the attention, he is not joyful for his father; instead he is sad for himself. Is it any wonder why he has no joy? He has no delight because he is totally self-centered rather than Father-centered. Realizing that salvation is meant to exalt the Savior will bolster our joy which comes from living all of our life centered on our Father. When we think God throws us parties because of our works, we have no parties to attend and we are joyless individuals. But if we know he throws parties because of his grace, we will have immense joy.

God's desire to exalt himself results in our salvation. His glory and our good are truly intertwined. When we are humble enough to allow him to have all the honor by relying on nothing but his grace, he is praised and we receive immense pleasure in him.

But he's not done exalting himself merely through our forgiveness. God's desire to show his awesomeness turns sinners into saints. He doesn't just display his everlasting power through our forgiveness, but also through our transformation.

10

More Than Forgiven

As long as you go on thinking about yourself like that and saying, "I'm not good enough; Oh, I'm not good enough," you are denying God – you are denying the gospel – you are denying the very essence of the faith and you will never be happy. -Dr. Martyn Loyd-Jones

I will give them an undivided heart and put a new spirit in them; I will remove from them their heart of stone and give them a heart of flesh. Then they will follow my decrees and be careful to keep my laws. They will be my people, and I will be their God. -Ezekiel 11:19-20

At the end of World War I, the victorious countries sought retribution from the losers, especially from Germany. As a way to punish the Germans, the victorious countries created the Treaty of Versailles. This treaty took away lands, profits, certain trading privileges, and much military freedom. It was so costly to the already defeated Germans that through the coming decades they would endure a dark economic depression.

As times grew harder and harder for the German people, they blamed the Treaty of Versailles more and more. Their animosity towards the world grew and they became very welcoming to any rising leaders who would stand up and defy the restrictions placed on them.

One leader seemed to capture the hearts of the people like no one else. His stirring speeches played on the peoples' discontentment and empowered them with bold, brash words. As he grew in power, he led the Nationalist Socialist Party towards complete control over all of Germany. Later he transformed this political entity into the Nazi Party. His name was Adolf Hitler and he was now Germany's supreme, tyrannical leader.

Most historians agree the penalties placed on Germany after losing World War I were a major contributor to what caused Hitler to rise to power and cause World War II. The people were so desperate to escape the penalties ruining their country, Hitler won their affection as he promised a stronger Germany unwilling to back down to anyone. When people are burdened by laws, rebellion always occurs.

When the Germans were again the losers in World War II, in the years to follow President Truman realized that if strict penalties were placed on Germany once more, Europe as a whole could never recover. He feared in the decades to follow another war caused by discontent Germans may become a real possibility. Therefore, instead of penalizing the Germans and making them open to help from America's enemies, the United States adopted the Marshal Plan. This plan purposefully did not take into account the past faults of Germany but sought only to help them create a different future.

Instead of seeking repayment from an already war-ravished nation, America gave resources. Instead of inflicting trade restriction, America sought to boost trade revenues in Germany. Instead of trying to totally destroy industry, they encouraged the modernization of German industry. And at least up to the time I am writing this book, the plan has seemed to work as there hasn't been a World War III.

While putting more burdens on an already defeated people always leads to more rebellion, empowering your defeated enemies, as counterintuitive as it may seem, leads to peace for many years to come. Things don't get better for any relationship if the loser is pushed down more and more by the winner. But when the one with power seeks to help the one without, both parties are benefitted.

All this reminds me of how the father treated the prodigal son. When the son came home, the father instantly forgave him. His forgiveness, however, did not demand that the father reinstate him again as a son. He could have forgiven him and then shook his head sympathetically as the son described his tale of woe.

After hearing about how the son realized his mistake in leaving, how he squandered his wealth in wild living, and how the famine was the final knockout blow, I think most people would have been backing up little by little as the son's explanation went on and on. Once the son finished his speech, with his eye's low to the ground in shame, most would probably respond with something like, "It's great to see you, son, and I'm really sorry all that happened, but . . . what do you want me to do about all that? I already gave you your inheritance. You chose your side. I forgive you, but I can't help with solving this problem you made."

But that's not what the father does. As John MacArthur explains in *The Prodigal Son*, before the son can even finish his speech, the father is already yelling for the servants to get him sandals, which in that day only the master and his heirs wore as the servants went barefoot. He calls for a robe, which only nobleman wore for the finest occasions, much like a tuxedo today. But he doesn't stop there, he even gives the son a family ring, which would be used in authenticating documents by pressing it into wax and then stamping the family crest, thus giving the son full authority again. Finally, he slaughters the fattened calf, a serious financial investment that would only be used for the most important family celebrations.[2]

The problem the son had was that he believed there was something better out there than the father's love. The father doesn't just forgive the son for this sin, he seeks to correct this problem from ever happening again by not only wiping the slate clean, but by giving the son these lavish gifts, proving his love is better than anything in the world.

The father explains the giving of these gifts with joy as he says, "For this son of mine was dead and is alive again . . ." (Luke 15:24). You see, he doesn't just forgive the son, he brings the son back to life. The son wasn't physically dead, but by leaving the way he did, the son was basically dead to the family. The father is the only one, therefore, who had the power to raise him from the dead by bringing him back into the family, just as Jesus is the only one who has the power to bring us back into the family of God.

Forgiveness is one of the greatest gifts God ever gives his people. Without it we would literally be doomed. It is also one of his greatest ways of exalting himself. But God seeks to show his greatness in more than forgiveness. He doesn't just want to wipe away our sins caused by our warring against him, he wants to make sure this war never happens again. He not only forgives, he raises us from the dead and gives us new life.

A Heart Problem Needs a Heart Solution

At the core of basic Christian beliefs is the idea that people do not sin and then become sinners, they sin because they are sinners. Over and over again the Bible points to the truth that apart from Jesus, the heart was born wicked and thus will produce wicked actions (Psalm 51:5, Matthew 7:17, Luke 6:45, John 15:5, Galatians 5:16-26).

There are many Christian books in our day describing what a Christian should be like, what we should be willing to give up, and what we should be willing to take on. If I'm being honest, the majority of this book has really only been that – a description of what we should do (which is to glorify God). These books are good. If we don't know what to do, how can we do it? But we can never stop with a sheer description of what a true Christian should be like. If we do, we are merely preaching morality, not true Christianity.

True Christianity not only tells you what you should do, it actually gives you the power to do it; and in some ways it even gives you the benefits of doing the right thing even when you don't do it. When someone tells me, "We as Christians need to love the world around us. We should pray for the person who annoys us at work. We should get in the slow lane to help us develop patience. We shouldn't be so hypocritical . . . ," obviously they are right (except for getting in the slow lane to develop patience; that's like telling an alcoholic to buy a bunch of booze and put it all over the house to make them stronger – that's just dumb).

However, they haven't helped me at all until they tell me how to do these things. Telling someone to be a good Christian without pointing them to the power of Christ is like telling a starving person not to be hungry but without giving them any food. If I am hungry, how can I not be hungry? That's my condition. That's what I currently am. That's why modern wisdom such as positive thinking eventually becomes ridiculous. "I'm not that hungry, I'm not that hungry . . . ." Telling yourself over and over again you're not hungry will work for about one day until your hunger just keeps getting worse and worse. Finally it will get so bad you'll break into the nearest bag of chips and devour the first box of Twinkies you come across, filling yourself with all the wrong types of foods.

That's what happens when you just try harder not to sin and be better. You eventually snap and fill yourself with junk. Problems don't go away. They need to be actively solved. If your heart's condition doesn't change, which is the real problem, you're not going to get different results by just trying harder to get different results. Who you are determines what you will do. And what you do is evidence and a reflection of who you really are (James 2:18). Until you begin to live from the new heart Jesus gave you by remaining in him, your sinful nature will continue to produce sin (John 15:5).

Charles Haddon Spurgeon, the man some people called the Prince of Preachers, said, "Repentance of the evil act, and not of the evil heart, is like men pumping water out of a leaky vessel, but forgetting to stop the leak. Some would dam up the stream, but leave the fountain still flowing; they would remove the eruption from the skin, but leave the disease in the flesh."[3]

Jesus doesn't just want to forgive, he wants to solve the problem that caused the sin in the first place. Like how America didn't just want to win the war but wanted to prevent another one from starting so they gave their former enemies assistance to rebuild, Jesus doesn't just pay our debts, he fills our account with all the resources we could ever need through the power of his Spirit inside of us (Ephesians 1:3). He doesn't leave us starving, expecting us to resist filling ourselves with sin. He fill us with good things so our new selves in him don't even want the junk (Psalm 103:5).

In Galatians 5:19 it says, "The acts of the sinful nature are obvious . . ." and then it goes on to list them. But then in verse 22 it says, "But the fruit of the Spirit is . . ." and then it lists those as well. Notice the sinful actions are attributed to our old-self controlled by the sinful nature. The good actions are *not* called "the fruit of the self-controlled Christian," or "the fruit of the sin management program," or "the fruit of the tips and techniques based in self-effort system." They're called "the fruit of the Spirit" because it's not the Christian producing them but God's Holy Spirit in the Christian.

When you're hungry, the only solution is to eat something. Perhaps that's why Jesus said he's the Bread of Life (John 6:35), because when you take his Spirit into your heart it actually gives you life, changing your sinful, hungry condition forever. Jesus knows that if we are the problem, we are not going to be the solution. John Stott in *Basic Christianity* recounts of Archbishop William Temple's explanation:

> It is no good giving me a play like Hamlet or
> King Lear, and telling me to write a play like

that. Shakespeare could do it; I can't. And it is not good showing me a life like the life of Jesus and telling me to live a life like that. Jesus could do it; I can't. But if the genius of Shakespeare could come and live in me, then I could write plays like that. And if the Spirit of Jesus could come and live in me, then I could live a life like that.[4]

Jesus is our example, but he's also more than that. He is the very power working in us to do what he commands. Psalm 86:11 states, "Teach me your way, LORD, that I may rely on your faithfulness; give me an undivided heart, that I may fear your name." We need to be taught God's ways, but we also need him to change our hearts so we can actually do what we are being taught.

The difference between justification and sanctification is that sanctification is the process by which we learn to live the life of a saint, even though that's what God has already made us into through our justification. After Jesus makes us into a new creation (justification), we still sin because we are now learning to live from that new nature (sanctification).

Hebrews 10:14 (ESV) explains "For by a single offering he has perfected for all time those who are being sanctified." We are both perfect and in the process of learning to live from that perfection. However, even as we learn to live from our justification, God deems us perfect and new no matter our past or future mistakes because our righteousness is all totally based upon the life of Christ applied to us (1 Corinthians 15:9-10).

Through justification, God not only acquits us of past, present, and future sins; he also accredits us with the righteousness and perfections of Jesus Christ. Jesus didn't die and rise from the grave to give us a second chance. He died to give us a new life that can never be taken away or stained in any way. Even after we sin, we are still a new creation because the perfect grace given to us was not given because of something we did, therefore it cannot be taken away by something we might do. "It is because of him that you are in Christ Jesus, who has become for us wisdom from God—that is, our righteousness, holiness and redemption. Therefore, as it is written: "Let the one who boasts boast in the Lord" (1 Corinthians 1:30-31).

God literally transfers Jesus' qualities to us (righteousness, holiness, and redemption) and thus we remain with these qualities even after we sin. As Paul wrote, "I no longer count on my own righteousness through obeying the law; rather, I become righteous through faith in Christ. For God's way of making us right with himself depends on faith" (Philippians 3:9 NLT). Jesus doesn't just give us a second chance because the amount of chances we have isn't our problem. It wasn't like we messed up by accident and maybe if we could get a "do-over" we might get it right next time. We don't need more chances. We need a sure thing, which is why God didn't give us back our old life but rather gave us a new life all together that can never be taken away.

We must continue to ask for forgiveness as we grow in sanctification, continuing to sin less and less (though in this life we will never be sinless); but our sin does not taint the new life within us (only our experience of it). Our sanctification should now actually be fueled by our justification. What Christ did in the past is now what gives me the means to live a glorifying life in the present and future. Because God accredits to me the perfections of Christ on a continual bases, I can grow towards perfection the rest of my life. My actions should reflect my ever deepening realization of who I truly am in Christ (Colossians 3:10). The more deeply and consistently I believe through faith what Christ has already made me into by grace, the more this reality will manifest into righteous living.

Our justification is what demands that our sanctification be genuine and present, meaning that there is actual growth in our lives and not just intellectual belief. If there is no evidence of sanctification, then the Bible says there was never truly justification (1 John 3:6). In Galatians 5:1 it says, "It is for freedom that Christ has set us free. Stand firm, then . . . ." It says Christ already "has" set the Christian free. Because we are free, Paul tells us we now have the power to live free. Because we are justified, we should also be showing evidence of being sanctified.

What Christ did on the cross took care of my sin and crucified my old nature (Romans 6:6). But what Christ did in the resurrection also gave me a new nature, "We were therefore buried with him through baptism into death in order that, just as Christ was raised from the dead through the glory of the Father, we too may live a new life" (Romans 6:4).

The only way to glorify God is through the power of God. It makes sense, doesn't it? If God truly wants all the glory, it should be no surprise that not only does he want us to honor him, he desires that we honor him through his power (Galatians 6:14). If I could glorify God in my own strength, then I would be worthy of praise. But he has made it so no one can have power but through him, so that no one can boast except in the work of Jesus Christ, which is the very power of God (1 Corinthians 1:18).

Our Diminishment Does Not Equate to His Magnification

Often times in our desire to give God all the praise, we seek to do this by diminishing ourselves. The desire to give all the credit to God is a holy desire, but the way we seek to fulfill this desire is often misguided.

People are often fearful of truly accepting how perfect, holy, and pure Jesus has really made them because they worry they are being prideful if they admit such things. Subconsciously we sometimes translates the words of John the Baptist, "He must become greater; I must become less," (John 3:30) into a verse that doesn't exist, "For him to become great I must make sure everyone knows I am a loser."

When John said what he did, he didn't mean for Jesus to be seen as great he must be seen as an idiot. What he meant was his publicity and fame needed to die down now that the real Star was here. John knew Jesus came to earth to show everyone how amazing he is so they would turn to him, benefitting themselves and praising God. And the way God shows the beauty of Jesus is by making it clear that Jesus deserves all the credit for everything good his people are doing. As John the Baptist explained, "A person can receive only what is given them from heaven" (John 3:27).

So we should seek to glorify God not by shining less, for as Saint Irenaeus stated, "The glory of God is man fully alive."

Rather, we should seek to glorify God by embracing his power so we are shining brighter while giving all the credit for our brightness to him.

An architect is praised because of the magnificent structures he creates. He isn't threatened that a building might get all the praise. Instead, he knows the more beautiful the building he makes, the more praise he will receive. If the building created itself, then it would be worthy of receiving praise. But a building is always made by a builder, just as a Christian is always made by Christ. We are not to boast, for we are God's workmanship (Ephesians 2:9-10).

When we become one with Christ, God doesn't tell us not to boast because there is nothing to boast about. He simply tells us not to boast because we don't deserve any of the credit. In fact, God actually expects us to boast about him, "Let him who boasts boast in the Lord" (1 Corinthians 1:30). He didn't say not to boast at all; he just said when you do boast, boast only in the Lord. This is why Paul says, "May I never boast except in the cross of our Lord Jesus Christ . . ." (Galatians 6:14). We are not supposed to diminish the amazing work of God in our hearts. We are supposed to fully recognize it and believe it so that we can praise God for it.

It's wrong to take credit for the goodness God produces in our lives, but it is also wrong to deny the goodness he produces. We are not to take recognition or deny the truth of what God has done for us. We are to accept his amazing grace as new creations and celebrate God because of it and through it. This doesn't diminish the works themselves. What we have is underserved, but it is also undiminished because Jesus transferred his worthiness to us. We don't deserve to be holy and free, but Jesus deserves for us to be holy and free because of the price he paid.

The gifts God gives us are not meant to make much of us. They are to make much of him. Wouldn't it be odd for a child to open all her presents on Christmas morning, have them all laid before her, then go into her room, look into the mirror, and give herself a high five for being so amazing at deserving such great gifts? The child would be totally missing the point. The people she should be thanking are her parents because they bought the gifts and freely gave them to her. Her parents are not trying to show her how much she deserves; they are trying to show her how much they love her. The child should know that without the parents she would have nothing.

She would have so little, she wouldn't even have any money to give gifts of her own to her parents. When little children want to buy their parents presents, they have to ask their parents for the resources to do it. If they hope to bless their parents, they first need to admit they have not the means on their own. The only way they can bless their parents is by asking the parents to give them the money to do it. And the parents freely give the child the money not because dad really wants another flashlight or another awful tie he can only where to family Christmas parties, and not because mom wants more plastic earrings or perfume that smells like grape juice. They give the child money so the child can buy them gifts because they know the greatest joy in life is not to receive but to give. The parents want to bless the child by giving him or her the greatest joy, the joy that can only come from pleasing those you love most. They show their love for their children by giving them the gift of giving.

This is exactly how it is with our heavenly Father and his children. We would have nothing to boast about if it wasn't for him, therefore we shouldn't boast about the gifts but rather about the Giver (James 1:17). And for us to really be able to please God, we must first know we cannot do it on our own (John 15:5). We must ask God to give us the power, and even the desire, to please him (Philippians 2:13). And he doesn't give us the means to please him because he needs more pleasure (he is perfectly happy within himself, Psalm 16:11), he gives us the means because his greatest act of love is helping us to love and give to him; for as Jesus himself said, "It is more blessed to give than to receive" (Acts 20:35). Therefore, he gives us the greatest gift of all: the gift of being able to please the One we love most. He gives us the gift of giving to him.

God forgives us for his glory, makes us new for his glory, and even causes us to produce good fruit for his glory. All of it benefits us, but it is all meant to glorify him.

11

Our Fruit Is for His Fame

This is to my Father's glory, that you bear much fruit, showing yourselves to be my disciples. -John 15:5, 8

Father, the hour has come. Glorify your Son, that your Son may glorify you. -John 17:1

One of the turning points in my life that caused me to stop being an English teacher and attend seminary happened during an event put on by an organization called Project Love. Every year about 2,000 students from varying schools in Cleveland go downtown for a massive, day-long seminar. Each year the guys at Project Love revolve this day around a positive characteristic. The event I attended with my students was called "Kickoff for Kindness."

As we entered the massive stadium, everywhere we looked there were banners and posters, "Be an agent of change!" "Be excellent in everything!" "Be kind to everyone!" All the speakers revolved their talks around the power one individual can have on the world simply through their personal kindness towards others. Their messages were well crafted, interesting, and even engaging for students to listen to, which was no easy task for my rowdy, inner-city bunch. But the main message of each speaker could be basically boiled down to this: Be a better person!

One speaker was talking about the issue of racism. With the microphone pressed tightly to his lips and with an intense look in his eyes, he yelled fervently to the crowd, "If you have a problem with skin color, get over it! Stop it! Be better than that!" The teachers and students cheered as he continued on in his passionate rant.

The visible effect of it all . . . zero. I was shocked that as we were leaving the stadium and piling into the busses, the students were being as cruel as ever. As it often happens with many inner-city gatherings, some kids were throwing up gang signs with their hands, aggressively eyeing the students from other schools, and looking for any way to express their dominance at someone else's expense. As I worked harder to try and keep control of my students, I found myself yelling at them in a desperate attempt to keep things under control.

As we made our way back to our school, amongst the debris flying out of the windows, screams going on behind me, and the general chaos that inevitably happens on a school bus, I stopped trying to control them and simply stared blankly at the seat in front of me. I leaned forward and pressed my forehead against its hot, sticky vinyl that smelled like . . . well, like a hot, sticky, vinyl school bus seat. I think the kid next to me was getting a little worried that I was legitimately losing my mind.

Remaining like that for the rest of the ride, allowing my head to roll back and forth against the seat as the bus bobbed up and down on the bumpy streets of Cleveland, I realized this job was really not for me. It wasn't that I wanted to run from a hard situation. God was truly teaching me a lot through this difficult job assignment. I finished out my commitment to the school and sought to show God's love in the situation he had placed me in, knowing if I wanted to move on, I had to first be willing to be faithful with the job I already had. But I also knew I had to move on because I wasn't able to endure any longer without being able to mention the name of Jesus.

I thank God for the people he has called and enabled to work in a secular setting. God uses teachers to change kids' lives for the better every day by displaying Christ in action and in words when the situation allows for it. God's plan to save the lost does not allow for all the Christians to run away and work with other Christians. But wherever God places us, he presents us with the world's problems not so we can tell people what they ought to do, but so we can show them and tell them about the one who can cause them to do it.

Project Love had a great message. The teachers I worked with had great messages every day for their students. They just couldn't do anything to empower the students to live the message out because they never pointed anyone to Jesus.

Jesus is the greatest teacher who ever lived. He was so great not simply because he told people what they should do, though he spent a lot of time doing that; he was the best because he was the only teacher to also give his students the power to do what he taught. He not only gave them that power, he was and is that power.

When Jesus Asks Us a Question, He Knows He Is the Answer

Jesus had some crazy teaching methods. Sometimes I wonder what he would do if he was a guest speaker at a seminar for kids. I can imagine him walking to the middle of the gym floor as the host has everyone welcome him with applause. Skipping the formalities of thanking everyone involved like all the other speakers do, I can see him immediately asking for a volunteer.

I imagine him picking some eager little 7th grader, probably because as the kid was yelling louder than everyone else he reminded Jesus of Peter. Perhaps Jesus would then ask what his name is, and then he would probably tell the crowd what his new name was. Jesus loved changing people's names when he met them. "You're name is Simon . . . that's cool, but I'm going to call you Peter." "What's that? Your name is Abram . . . . I'd rather call you Abraham instead."

With all the thousands of students and teachers watching Jesus and his newly renamed volunteer at center floor of the gym, waiting to see what's going to happen next, I picture Jesus bringing the microphone up to his mouth and saying two words to his volunteer which echo throughout the stadium, "Feed them."

Perhaps a moment of silence would go by before the people would begin to whisper in confusion to one another, "Did he just tell that kid to feed us?" To clear up any confusion, I imagine Jesus saying it again, but this time with a slight rising of the eye brow and a gentle pat on the back of his speechless helper, "Go on, feed them."

Maybe now the host would come back smiling and nervously usher Jesus off the floor, "Okay kids . . . um, let's give this crazy man a big round of applause." Or maybe Jesus would see some student eating some nachos and decide to cut right to the chase and then he would multiply the nachos. Everyone would be staring back oddly at Jesus, "That was a weird trick," some might say, "but hey, we all got some free nachos out of it."

As fun (or odd, if you don't get my sense of humor) as it may be to think about what Jesus would do if he was before a crowd of thousands, we don't really need to. The account of Jesus feeding the five-thousand is one of his most well-known miracles as it is one of the only miracles recorded in all four gospels. In John 6:5-6 it states, "When Jesus looked up and saw a great crowd coming toward him, he said to Philip, 'Where shall we buy bread for these people to eat?' He asked this only to test him, for he already had in mind what he was going to do."

Before Jesus even asked the disciples to give the people something to eat, he already was planning on providing the food himself. So why does he ask them in the first place?

He doesn't present them with this challenge to toy with them; verse 5 says he did it to test them. He wants to know what will happen if he asks them to do something ridiculously difficult. I say "difficult" and not "impossible" because the disciples had already come up with a plan on how they could actually do this. They didn't like their own plan, but they did have one. Mark 6:37 states, "They said to him, 'That would take more than half a year's wages! Are we to go and spend that much on bread and give it to them to eat?'"

If Jesus wanted them to produce good fruit (good actions) in their own strength, he would have said, "Yeah, go buy it." The disciples obviously had the money, that's why they were getting so nervous. They were concerned that they might actually have to spend it. There were times when Jesus condoned the use of personal resources for the sake of his

Kingdom (John 12:7), but I believe he was trying to teach a deeper lesson at this time.

He was trying to teach them the lesson that when God asks you do something, he's not asking you to do it in your own strength. Jesus really did want the disciples to feed the people – as we will see when Jesus gives the food to them to then give to the people – but he also wanted them to use his power to do it. It was as if he was presenting them with a near impossible challenge to show how little power they had without him. When Andrew came up to Jesus, he asked, "Here is a boy with five small barley loaves and two small fish, but how far will they go among so many?" (John 6:9).

I like how there is such an emphasis on it being a "boy" (not a man) with five "small" (not big) loaves and two "small" fish followed with the question, "but how far will they go among so many?" It is as if when John is writing this he is really stressing how little chance they had at doing what Jesus wanted in their own strength. I love it! As all the grown men are sitting around trying to solve this problem, it's a little kid who is starting to understand what Jesus is trying to teach them.

When directed to love thy neighbor, the adults are looking to themselves. This child, however, is looking to Jesus. When Jesus takes the boy's lunch his mommy probably packed for him early that day, I wonder if he was shaking his head at his grown up disciples and saying with his actions, "You should be ashamed of yourselves, letting this little boy have more faith than you all, my mighty twelve. Let me show you what I can do when someone is actually trusting in my power, even if all he has is a little lunch packed by his mother."

By rejecting their offer to do it in their own strength and then by taking the offer of a little boy who so foolishly offered up his meager little lunch to Jesus, he is showing everyone that it's not about how little or much you have, it's about how much of it you are going to give to him. Jesus is teaching the disciples that him plus a little boy with faith is thousands of times more powerful than the disciples trying to do things on their own.

The text also emphasizes the amount the child gave to Jesus. Five loaves plus two fish equals seven. On a different occasion when Jesus feeds the four thousand the text makes it clear there were "seven" loaves and a "few small fish" (Matthew 15:34). Both accounts of the two miracles where Jesus multiplies a little food into a lot emphasize the number seven. In the Bible, seven is often the number of completion. The message is pretty clear. No matter how little you have, when you give it all to Jesus, it is always completely enough. Jesus is pointing out that when he asks us to do something, he wants us to rely on his power to do it. It didn't really matter what the disciples had. Jesus could have rained down bread from the sky if he wanted to just like he did for the Israelites with the manna.

Remember, he asks them the question of how they are going to feed all these people to test them. Every question God brings into our lives is meant for the same reason. God doesn't ask us to produce loving actions because he needs them; he asks us to do loving things to see if we will turn to him first to do them. When Jesus asked the disciples to feed the thousands and they said all they had was five loaves and two fish, that wasn't true. They had Jesus right by their side. He was testing them, hoping they would say, "We can't do it! But you can! Here's all we have. Do with it what you want."

Our fruit is supposed to be for his fame because he is the only one who has the power to produce it through us. God asks us to do important things for him but always expects us to rely on him to do it. He gives us missions that seem impossible so he has the opportunity to display his power through us for the whole world to see how good he is.

After Jesus multiplied the little boy's food, Matthew 14:19 states, "Then he gave [the fish and bread] to the disciples, and the disciples gave them to the people." That's always the pattern God desires for our good works. He gives to us; we are to then give it to others. So when Jesus asks us, "What do you have to give these people in need?" our answer should be, "Nothing, except what you give us!"

Acts 17:25 states, "And he is not served by human hands, as if he needed anything. Rather, he himself gives everyone life and breath and everything else." Psalm 50:12 says, "If I were hungry I would not tell you, for the world is mine, and all that is in it."

David understood this, for as his life was drawing to an end and he was dedicating material to the Lord to build the temple, he prayed to God with confidence before the great assembly, "But who am I, and who are my people, that we should be able to give as generously as this? Everything comes from you, and we have given you only what comes from your hand" (1 Chronicles 29:14).

God states his motive clearly in Ezekiel 36:23, "Then the nations will know that I am the LORD, declares the Sovereign Lord, when I show myself holy though you before their eyes." God grants us a holiness that benefits us, but he does it to exalt himself before the whole world.

God doesn't need our service. He desires to display his majesty by giving us the power to do what he commands, and as tempting as it is to take the credit, we must resist. C.S. Lewis states, "It is easy to acknowledge, but almost impossible to realize for long, that we are mirrors whose brightness, if we are bright, is wholly derived from the sun that shines upon us."[1]

God gives the orders, he supplies the means to accomplish them, and therefore he deserves all the praise (John 3:21). And those who recognize this are the ones given the most power.

Powerful People Give Credit to God

It's my belief that the amount of real spiritual power someone has is equal to how much credit they are willing to give God in their hearts and actions. God greatly uses those who are finally ready to give him all the glory. If you still desire the praise, then God isn't going to curse you with the power.

This trait of possessing power and yet knowing it comes from God is always present in those God uses the most. Joseph is a perfect example of this. Joseph was successful in all that he did because the Lord made him successful. His brothers could get jealous of the coat his father made him, sell him to some merchants, and thus take away his place in the family (Genesis 37). Potiphar's wife could take Joseph's cloak as a way to frame him and tell her husband Joseph tried to rape her, thus ruining his career as the assistant to Pharaoh's captain of the guard (Genesis 39). (As a side note, Joseph seriously needs to stop accessorizing so much. This is now the second time his clothing has got him in a mess.) The cupbearer could forget to repay Joseph for interpreting his dream by not telling Pharaoh of Joseph's innocence, thus making Joseph stay in prison for another two years (Genesis 40).

But what no one could do was take the presence of God away from him, thus everywhere Joseph went he was still successful despite difficult circumstances. It wasn't because Joseph had so much skill that he found favor with everyone and was so amazing in all he did. God was responsible for it all. When he was with his family, God caused his father to love Joseph more because of the miracle of Joseph's birth to his dad in old age (Genesis 37:3). When he was sold into Potiphar's house, it says, "The Lord was with Joseph and he prospered . . ." (Genesis 39:2). When he went to the jail, it says, "The warden paid no attention to anything under Joseph's care, because the Lord was with Joseph and gave him success in whatever he did" (Genesis 39:23).

Not only was God responsible for Joseph's success and power, Joseph knew it, which freed God to give him more. When Joseph finally was remembered by the cupbearer and summoned before Pharaoh to interpret his dream, Joseph didn't crack under the brightest lights he'd seen so far. If he was ever going to take credit for the power God gave him, now would be the time to do it. Standing before the most powerful person in Egypt and with all the royal officials looking on, this would have been the perfect setting for Joseph to exalt himself.

In Genesis 41:15 we have Pharaoh setting Joseph up for a prideful fall before God, "Pharaoh said to Joseph, 'I had a dream, and no one can interpret it. But I have heard it said of you that when you hear a dream you can interpret it." But Joseph passes the test and responds immediately with, "I cannot do it, but God will give Pharaoh the answer he desires" (Genesis 41:16). Because Joseph could be trusted to glorify God with the gifts he already had, God blessed Joseph with even more power (Genesis 41:39-40). God uses us in significant ways when we are ready to admit before all how useless we are without him.

Joseph was truly a God-centered, glory-giving man of God. He had every opportunity to stop God midway through the process. Through anyone of the many difficult external circumstances he endured, Joseph could have turned from God and thus totally missed out on the finished work of art God was creating. But he trusted the faithfulness of God even when life didn't make sense. He was faithful to give God the glory for the little God gave him, so God knew Joseph would give him the glory if he blessed him with much (Luke 16:10). As Proverbs 27:21 (NLT) states, "Fire tests the purity of silver and gold, but a person is tested by being praised."

Because he gave God all the credit and allowed God to finish what he had been planning to do from the start, just like how Jesus had a plan from the start for multiplying the food (John 6:6), Joseph enjoyed the pleasure of God producing good through him. Because he was willing to turn to God for the power, Joseph, like the little boy who offered up his lunch, was used by God to help thousands (Genesis 41:53-57).

As this drama involving Joseph came to end, he was able to say with confidence to the very people who tried to hurt him, "You intended to harm me, but God intended it for good to accomplish what is now being done, the saving of many lives" (Genesis 50:20).

By the grace of God Joseph understood what it took to possess the power of God. First, he needed God to be the one producing the power in his life; second, he needed to give God all the glory for producing this power in his life; and third, he needed to know that this power was meant for the benefit of others for the sake of God's exaltation.

God wants us to produce fruit through and for this glory. But the fruit he cares most about is loving people.

12

Filled to Love

You will never make a good impression on other people until you stop thinking about what sort of impression you are making. -C.S. Lewis[1]

For what we preach is not ourselves, but Jesus Christ as Lord, and ourselves as your servants for Jesus' sake. -2 Corinthians 4:5

In the last chapter we learned whenever God asks us to do something, he expects us to rely on him to do it. Additionally, God knows we are only ready to be used greatly by him when we are ready to give him all the credit. And when God does use us in significant ways, it is always expressed through our service to other people.

The disciples totally missed this lesson before they received the power of the Holy Spirit at Pentecost in Acts 2. Before the Holy Spirit entered them, they were arguing about who was the greatest (Luke 9:46), jockeying for positions of authority in Jesus' Kingdom (Matthew 20:21), and desiring to use the power of God to call down bolts of fire to punish those disgusting Gentiles they despised (Luke 9:54). But once the Holy Spirit entered them, changing them from the inside out, then they had the power to actually do what Jesus taught. As Oswald Chambers put it, "Pentecost did not teach the disciples anything; it made them the incarnation of what they preached."[2]

In Acts 3 Peter and John are approached by a crippled beggar who had been that way since birth. When he sees them, he asks for money as he always did of those passing by. I wonder when his question was posed to Peter and John if they gave each other that look which didn't need any words, that look only longtime friends who had been through a lot together could have understood, "Are you thinking what I'm thinking?" When the man asked them for something they were unable to do in their own strength, I imagine them both thinking of the time Jesus asked them to feed the five-thousand.

But this time, instead of complaining and getting all worked up because of the difficulty of the situation, they put into practice what Jesus was trying to teach them on that memorable day before thousands of hungry people – that when God gives you a task to accomplish, he expects you to rely on him for the power to do it so he will receive all the praise. Verse 6 states, "Then Peter said, 'Silver or gold I do not have, but what I do have I give you. In the name of Jesus Christ of Nazareth, walk.'" Jesus must have been smiling when he saw this. They got it, they finally passed the test. Instead of taking a collection or thinking of some clever way they could help this guy in their own strength, when presented with a problem they turned to Jesus for the solution.

Not only did they rely on the power of God to glorify him, they gave him all the credit as well. As the people were getting ready to exalt them for this miracle, Peter said to them (Acts 3:12), "Fellow Israelites, why does this surprise you? Why do you stare at us as if by our own power or godliness we had made this man walk?"

To top it all off, the disciples started preaching a message to the Jews that explained just as the power they received benefited this beggar, the covenant promise the Jews received was actually meant to benefit the whole world (Acts3:25), "Through your offspring all peoples on earth will be blessed."

Now, because they had been changed from the inside out by the Holy Spirit, instead of trying to call down bolts of fire to destroy the Gentiles, they were preaching to the Jews how God has actually planned to bless Israel so the Jews can be a blessing to the whole world through the Messiah, Jesus, who offers salvation to all.

They finally understood God's desire for them. Jesus gave them power so they could use it for the benefit of others for the honor of God. For just as God doesn't love us simply for us but also for his glory, he desires that we love people not just to love them but to show God's grandeur.

Loving people glorifies God because only through his power are we truly able to love (2 Corinthians 9:12-15). Over and over again in Scripture God desires to show his love to the world by expressing it though his people, "Live such good lives among the pagans that, though they accuse you of doing wrong, they may see your good deeds and glorify God on the day he visits us. . . . For it is God's will that by doing good you should silence the ignorant talk of foolish people" (1 Peter 2:12, 15).

People often come to know God when we love them because deep down they understand this true love can only be the result of Jesus Christ working through us. People know people are not naturally loving. So when a Christian expresses real love, people know it is because the only true God is working through the Christian (Galatians 5:6).

The world is not unified and the world knows it, so when they see true unity they must attribute it to something greater than people. In John 17:22-23 Jesus prayed to his Father regarding his future followers, "I have given them the glory that you gave me, that they may be one as we are one— I in them and you in me—so that they may be brought to complete unity. Then the world will know that you sent me . . . ."

Nothing gives God more recognition than when his people love other people because everyone knows he deserves all the credit for this. And since God's glory and our good our intertwined, not only is God glorified when we love people, the way we love people is to glorify God.

The common gut reaction to placing God above everyone else is that this means we are not free to love humans. However, putting the glory of God above everyone else does not contradict the command to love people, for it is actually the very thing that makes it possible. In reality, the most loving think you can do for anyone is to love God more than them.

Being Free From Idolatry Is Being Free to Love

Jesus was always a constant, giving people what they needed, which was not always what they wanted from him. He healed, cursed, discipled, disciplined, rebuked, encouraged, served, and allowed himself to be worshipped. He gave whatever the moment needed. The only reason he was free to love so recklessly was because he wasn't afraid of losing the praise of people. He was so concerned with the glory of God he wasn't concerned with his perception before the masses. Because his relationship with his Father was secure, he was free to love people even if they hated him for it.

If the praise of people, however, was Jesus' main motivation in loving them, he would have been parallelized every time he tried: "I wonder if I heal this guy on the Sabbath if they will hate me?" "I wonder if I turn these massive jugs of water into wine if people will think I am a drunk?" "I wonder if I don't stick up for myself if everyone will think I am actually guilty of some sin worthy of this crucifixion I am going to endure for them?"

If Jesus was not most concerned with the glory of God, he would not have been free to love as he did when on earth. Jesus knew it wasn't a matter of "if" his earthly relationships would become hurtful and broken, it was simply a matter of "when." C.S. Lewis states:

> To love at all is to be vulnerable. Love anything and your heart will be wrung and possibly broken. If you want to make sure of keeping it intact you must give it to no one, not even an animal. Wrap it carefully round with hobbies and little luxuries; avoid all entanglements. Lock it up safe in the casket or coffin of your selfishness. But in that casket, safe, dark, motionless, airless, it will change. It will not be broken; it will become unbreakable, impenetrable, irredeemable. To love is to be vulnerable.[3]

To love you must not be paralyzed from the fear of being hurt. And the only way you can be free from the fear of pain caused by people is to not make them your ultimate joy. People will hurt us. Unlike the movies, perfect people do not exist; therefore perfect relationships do not exist. The only way to continue to love in a dysfunctional relationship – which is every human relationship to some degree – is to have something greater than this relationship which will keep you afloat even when all else fails. Only when we are totally secure in God, filled with his love, are we free to love and be vulnerable with the people we know will one day hurt us. If you don't seek to love God as your highest aim in every relationship you have, these relationships will not last. You can't love someone you are idolizing. Nobody is perfect except Christ. If we expect the ones we love to be perfect, our love will quickly turn to hate.

This is why so many romantic relationships have such extremes. One day they both feel the other is an angel from heaven and the next they are both totally convinced the other is the antichrist. Why? Because false gods never matchup with the real thing.

When what we need is Jesus, the only perfect person, but what we have is a fallen individual like ourselves, we become angry with them because they do not fill us as our hearts desire. If we try to love people based on their merit, we fail miserably because their merit fails us miserably. The higher we elevate someone, the farther they are going to fall. You can always know how much you idolized another person by how mad you are when they eventually disappoint you.

Whatever you worship is what you give power over you. When people are your gods, then they are the ones who control you. If people have the power over your happiness, then people, not God, will have the power over your unhappiness. Whatever you give the power to make you feel strong, you also give the power to make you feel weak. Whatever you give the power to fill you, you also give the power to make you empty. Only God is worthy of such power because only God can love us perfectly. People should be important to us and the cause of much joy, but they shouldn't be our ultimate anything.

Unless we love God more than people, our love for them will eventually turn to hate. One extreme example of this involves Amnon and Tamar. Amnon was totally obsessed with beautiful Tamar. He had idolized her until he couldn't take it anymore. He wanted to sleep with her before marriage but she resisted him, "But he refused to listen to her, and since he was stronger than she, he raped her. Then Amnon hated her with intense hatred. In fact, he hated her more than he had loved her" (2 Samuel 13:14-15).

After Amnon tried to use Tamar to fill himself and it didn't work, he became angry with her because he felt she let him down when his idolized fantasy of her did not quench his inner needs. He had thought Tamar was the perfect person he had always been looking for, and since he elevated her so high he despised her all the more when reality came knocking. Because Amnon "loved" her more than he loved God, he wasn't able to love her at all.

Joseph, on the other hand, loved God more than Potiphar's wife so he was able to resist her seduction and love her well. Over and over again she kept trying to lure Joseph to her, but he resisted every time. When she finally got him alone and was forcing his hand, Joseph responds to her temptations with a truly revealing statement, "How then could I do such a wicked thing and sin against God?" (Genesis 39:9).

He doesn't say he wasn't attracted to her. He doesn't explain how he couldn't do this to Potiphar because he loved Potiphar so much for all that he had done for Joseph. He doesn't say he values her too much to use her in that way. When his back was finally against the wall, the only thing that kept him strong was his greater passion for God over people. He could run from temptation, love Potiphar, love Potiphar's wife, and love all those in his life who misused him because he loved God more than them.

Over and over again in the Bible you see this quality in those God uses greatly. They are able to love others so well because they love God the most. After they had received the Holy Spirit and Peter and the other apostles were being persecuted for preaching Christ, their response was simple, "We must obey God rather than human beings!" (Acts 5:29). Because they sought to glorify God above everything else, they were able to love the people by preaching Jesus even though these were the very ones persecuting them for it.

In Jesus we can see most clearly this quality of being free to love others because his deepest love is for his Father. There is only one story in the whole Bible regarding Jesus' boyhood (Luke 2:41-52). In this story his parents lose track of him. When they find him in the temple they are upset and question why he did this to them. He responds, "Didn't you know I had to be in my Father's house?" (verse 49). It then says, "Then he went down to Nazareth with them and was obedient to them" (verse 51).

I believe this is the only story about Jesus' boyhood because it's the only one we need. Here we learn that even at a young age Jesus knew his greatest devotion was to be towards his Father. And because he loved his Father more and was more obedient to him than to his earthly parents, this is the very thing that enabled him to love and obey his parents so well.

Jesus could continue on despite the disapproval of those closest to him (Mark 3:21, 31-34), he could correct his friends when they got out of line even though it made it awkward (Mark 8:33), he could tell his fans what they needed to hear even though he knew they would leave him for it (John 6:60-66), he could love sinners by dying for them even though they were the very ones pounding in the nails (Luke 23:34) – he could love all people the way they needed to be loved because his greatest desire was to honor God.

If being nice was needed, Jesus could make Mr. Rogers look like a novice. If firmly rebuking someone was needed, Jesus could have scared the courage out of General Custard himself. He was not controlled by the fear of people because people were not his god. He could love them even when they hated him because his motivation was ultimately rooted in his desire to please his Father. Because his Father's glory was his highest aim, he was free to arrange for our greatest good despite what it might cost him, knowing we would never be able to pay him back.

To love others well we must realize it is not wrong or sinful to have people in the world that do not like us. You can't love someone you are idolizing, you will simply be led astray by them, trying to be their friend at whatever cost to your own detriment. We will laugh at jokes we shouldn't, accept invitations to parties we knows will bring us harm, and we will compromise ourselves so often we will become bewildered to where our true allegiance lies. And ironically enough, the freer we are from seeking people's approval of us, the more they are usually drawn to us anyway. But even if they aren't, when God is our highest aim, our lives won't be in shambles if someone dislikes us.

Only when our hearts are right with God will we be able to serve and not take, love and not idolize, forgive and not resent, respect and not dishonor. When God's praise becomes our highest pleasure, we are free to give undeserved love to others. We will truly love others despite what it might cost us only when we are totally fulfilled in him. We mustn't love people to fill ourselves, for we will only be free to love others when we are already filled.

Loving People Out of Our Love for God

Our good and his glory are intertwined because when we are satisfied with pleasing him above others, we are fulfilled and thus free to enjoy people for who they are rather than despise them for who they are not. Even when people are undeserving, we can still love them because God is always deserving. When God is our motivation to love others because it pleases him, we will always have the fuel to love. But if people are our motivation, our desire to love them will fail and fade the more they do not live up to our demands.

Whenever I am involved in a speaking engagement, I am keenly aware that my motivation to love the people I am speaking to cannot be based in their approval of me. If I get on stage and want something from the people I am supposed to be serving (claps, laughs, interested looks on their faces, est.) when they don't give these things to me my motivation to love them vanishes. I can't expect to take from those I am trying to impart something to. And to have anything to truly give, I must first get it from God. I must always seek to serve out of my fullness rather than my emptiness. I must be full of God's love so I then have a love to give away.

Paul says, "And a person with a changed heart seeks praise from God, not from people" (Romans 2:29 NLT). Not only should we love people because it's the right thing to do, we should love others because that's the type of person we are in Christ.

This reminds me of the time I had been counseling a woman who was getting older in age but was yet to be married. Having been given the opportunity to watch her interact in real life, she asked me if there was anything I saw about her that might be hindering her chances with men. Feeling the most loving thing to do was to tell her the truth, I decided to go for it even though she might punch me in the face afterwards, "Well," I said after one more hard swallow, "honestly, you are actually pretty disrespectful towards guys. I don't think you mean to do this, but when a man feels disrespected it is a big turn off."

"You're right," she said without hesitation. I was a bit surprised that she knew this about herself so I prodded further. As I continued my questions she confided that she was disrespectful to the men in her life because they deserved it. Her boss was a jerk, her dad was insensitive, and the guys she was friends with at church liked to make fun of her.

I couldn't argue with these points. It was all true. But it was also true that her disrespectfulness was a serious turnoff to every other guy she came in contact with. And then a sentence just popped out of me I'm sure was the Lord's doing, "You shouldn't seek to respect men because they deserve it. You should respect them because that's the type of woman God has made you to be."

That line instantly resonated with her. "You're so right!" she exclaimed. "I've been treating guys like dirt because I know eventually they will all deserve it. But if I hope to be married one day, I better stop ruining my chances by giving everyone what they deserve. Heck, I hope my husband doesn't always treat me like I deserve. I'm kind of crazy sometimes . . . ."

We cannot treat people fairly. Christ tells us to love others as he has loved us (John 13:34), and he does not love us as we deserve (Psalm 103:10). His love is far greater than anything we ought to have. If we all got what we deserved in our relationships with others, no one would have any relationships. Perhaps this is why Paul instructs, "Make sure that nobody pays back wrong for wrong . . ." (1 Thessalonians 5:15). Paying back wrong for wrong is fair, but it will lead to a miserable life. People who enjoy life the most are the ones who love deeply, but not because their friends, family, and co-workers are more loveable and just better people than everyone else in the world; they love more because they are more loving.

God desires that we love unconditionally not because people deserve it, but because that's the type of person he has created us to be in Christ. We are to reflect him now. He loved us because he is love, not because we were lovable. We are now to forgive because we have a forgiving nature. We are to serve because we have a servant's heart. We are to be a light to a dark world because the Light of Life is within us.

When our relationship with God is central, he changes us through his power into loving people.

13

Not the Means . . . the End

Abandon any other concern, including any special devotions you've undertaken simply as a means to an end. God is our "end." If we are diligently practicing His presence, we shouldn't need our former "means." -Brother Lawrence[1]

One thing I ask from the LORD; this only do I seek: that I may dwell in the house of the LORD all the days of my life, to gaze on the beauty of the LORD and to seek him in his temple. - Psalm 27:4

When I first met my wife, she was from North Carolina and I was from Ohio, but we both found ourselves in Liberia, West Africa on a missions trip. We started off just as friends, but those around us knew something more was eventually going to happen. When we were in a room of people or on some crazy adventure with a group of friends, everyone teased us on how we ignored those around us. We didn't mean to neglect our other friends, but we brought each other so much joy we couldn't really help it.

She would laugh at my jokes a little longer than everyone else, I listened a little closer to her whenever she would have something to say in the group, and whenever there was a mass of people sitting down, it seemed we magnetically found two seats right next to each other.

When my time was over in Africa, however, I honestly thought I'd never see her again. As my last day in Liberia neared to an end, we spent every last minute enjoying each other. I was only nineteen at the time, but I had been through enough life experiences that I knew these magical friendships usually fade just as quickly as they come.

When you travel together on the streets of a third-world country, care for orphans together, grieve together over the tragedies that occur on the mission field, and experience things no one back home will understand, it takes the friendship to an entirely different level. So I just assumed when these whimsical experiences were over and we were both back in our different states with our different friends living our different lives, our relationship would simply regress to a few faded pictures looked at with fond memories.

But when we both got home, that's not what happened. We started doing little reunion trips. We gathered up in West Virginia to go white water rafting and invited whoever could make it. Sure it was only a two-and-half month reunion and only two other friends could come, but we continued planning these little trips, using whatever excuse we could to be together.

Despite all the complications we both saw with us being together, we decided this "friend thing" just wasn't cutting it anymore. Within about a year and half we were married.

Through this whole experience of discovering how much we enjoy each other, neither of us ever questioned the other person's motivation due to the personal satisfaction we found in one another. I never thought she was selfish for enjoying my jokes more than other people did. She never thought I was self-centered because I sought to bring pleasure to myself by saving her a seat right next to me. Neither of us questioned the sincerity of the other's devotion due to the motive of personal happiness we both found from being connected to the other.

Now that we are married, own a house together, have children, and basically share everything we own, neither of us are wondering if our history was simply a grand plan to manipulate the other to get these things. Our marriage has brought us each many blessings, but our relationship with one another was never about these things. It was never a means to end. The relationship was and is an end in itself. I didn't want Bethany because I wanted these blessings. Simply being with her has been the best blessing of all.

Sadly, this doubt of motivation is what often hinders our relationships with God. We think to truly love and glorify him, we must be totally sterile of any self-benefitting. We think if we are seeking him because he makes us happy or brings us peace, we do not really love God because we have our own happiness in mind. Thankfully, that's not how God views it. Rather, when he becomes are ultimate treasure and joy, only then is he most glorified in our lives.

When Bethany and I find immense joy in each other, we don't question the other person's love. We actually feel the most loved when we experience the other person's delight in us. Personal delight in someone other than yourself is not selfish, it is the highest form of love. As John Piper has explained so concisely in his book *Desiring God*, "God is most glorified in us when we are most satisfied in him."[2]

God Is the Goal of Seeking God

We need not fear our pursuit of pleasure in God is wrong. If we sought pleasure by any means in any source, this would be wrong. But when I seek pleasure *in God*, this benefits me and glorifies him.

This book has been about discovering the key to finding joy despite personal difficulties by seeing everything through the lens of God's glory. This is not a selfish pursuit because when we seek pleasure in God, he is our aim, our treasure, our highest love.

John Piper's statement that "God is most glorified in us when we are most satisfied in him" is the foundation to what I have been trying to explain throughout this book, which is that we are most satisfied in God when he is most glorified in us. Because God is glorified through our joy in him, it is right to seek our joy in him. Because our satisfaction in God glorifies him, it is right to seek to glorify him for the satisfaction in him.

God tells us to put all earthly pursuits behind us and to seek him only, not for the sake of suffering but for the sake of our deepest satisfaction in him. We are to give up the plastic necklace for a string of real pearls, leaving the lesser to gain the greater. Some might think seeking our own good cheapens our love for God. This would be true if it were not for the fact that the real reward we seek from God is God. We don't seek to put on just any jewelry to make ourselves a beautiful bride, we seek to put on God himself to make ourselves beautiful and to magnify him (Jeremiah 2:32). As C.S. Lewis wrote, "Your real, new self will not come as long as you are looking for it. It will come when you are looking for Him."[3]

Seeking to please God does not lead to a destination; this journey is the destination. God is not a means to an end; he is the end in which we seek. God himself is our prize, for he would never allow anything to be better than himself.

Love is not something God has. Love is who God is. Therefore God always offers himself as the ultimate gift of love. Hebrews 11:6 explains further, "And without faith it is impossible to please God, because anyone who comes to him must believe that he exists and that he rewards those who earnestly seek him." Put plainly, it pleases God to reward us with himself when we seek him in faith, for the rewards of God are always more of God because this benefits us and glorifies him.

The most glorifying life you can live is when you fully enjoy a life of glorifying God, thus we should seek maximum personal joy in God because this is what honors him most. God is not most pleased when we serve him but when we serve him and enjoy it, "for God loves a cheerful giver" (2 Corinthians 9:7). Jonathan Edwards states, "God is glorified not only by His glory's being seen, but by its being rejoiced in. When those that see it delight in it, God is more glorified than if they only see it."[4]

In fact our service to God is not complete until we do enjoy him because God commands us to do this, "Rejoice in the Lord always. I will say it again: Rejoice!" (Philippians 4:4). Again in 1 Thessalonians 5:16-18 we see what God's will is for us, "Rejoice always, pray continually, give thanks in all circumstances; for this is God's will for you in Christ Jesus." God actually punishes the Israelites because they had no "awe" of him (Jeremiah 2:19) and because they forsook him for gods who could not satisfy them like he could (Jeremiah 2:13). Therefore our obligation to obey the commands of God and our delighting in the Lord are not two different pursuits but one.[5] We are commanded to find pleasure in him and this "burden" is our greatest delight and privilege.

The Goal of the Gospel Is God

If finding joy in God is what most glorifies him, then how do we find joy in him? There are countless ways to find joy in God, but to simplify it in a big way: Ultimately, our greatest joy stems from being in his presence, "You make known to me the path of life; in your presence there is fullness of joy; at your right hand are pleasures forevermore" (Psalm 16:11).

When we were visiting Bethany's grandma years ago, on her windowsill she had this tacky trinket that said, "Joy is not the absence of suffering but being in the presence of the Lord." The trinket may have been tacky but its message was profound. Grandma is full of joy but her husband was not. He suffered from fits of rage and depression triggered by an abusive childhood and his painful memories of World War II. Through all the verbal abuse he put her through, she cared for him right up to the day of his death, attending his every need as he lay helplessly in bed. She had a long, hard life with this man, but she is still overflowing with joy. She is truly one of the happiest people I know. Surely this is due to the presence of God, not her external circumstances.

God is maximally pleased with us when we are in awful circumstances but still have immense joy in him; and equally so, he is maximally pleased with us when we are in amazing circumstances and yet do not have joy for any other reason than because we have him (the true gift of the material blessing is that it reminds us of our generous heavenly Father). When we have fullness of joy in him no matter the circumstance, it shows how wonderful and awesome he is. His presence is our ultimate pleasure, so we can have this immense joy at all times since we can be in his presence at all times because of what Jesus did in the gospel.

We could never come into the presence of God without his grace expressed in what Christ did through the gospel. The gospel is the good news of what Jesus did on behalf of sinners, mainly in the form of what he accomplished through his death and resurrection (1 Corinthians 15:3-4).

The gospel enhances the beauty of God to a watching world because through it he is seen as the ultimate prize. The end goal of the gospel is God. The gospel magnifies the infinite worth of God because the death and resurrection of Jesus, the most sacrificial and powerful acts ever done, were accomplished so people would be able to know and enjoy God intimately.

If such a sacrifice was paid and such power was displayed for people to be with God, he must be the most glorious person in the entire universe. Jesus proclaimed in his prayer on our behalf, "Now this is eternal life: that they know you, the only true God, and Jesus Christ, whom you have sent" (John 17:3). The gospel's offer of eternal life is actually an offer to intimately knowing God, the ultimate destination.

Therefore, we should offer people the gospel more than everything else we offer them because the gospel glorifies God more than anything else we could ever offer. The gospel is the apex of Christ's love, and Christ is the apex image of the invisible God (2 Corinthians 4:4). This means that what we know about God can be seen most clearly in Christ. And what we know about Christ can be seen most clearly in the gospel. Therefore, if we desire to reflect God, the gospel message should dominate what Christians show the world.

The gospel is not a means to salvation, justification, a fruitful life, power in prayer, or anything else but to God himself. Salvation saves us . . . for an eternal relationship with God. We are justified . . . so we can commune with God. We are given the power to produce fruit . . . to please God. We are given the ability to pray . . . so we can actively be in the joy-producing presence of God. We are to spend our lives enjoying him because this glorifies God. Every blessing from him finds its true purpose in him. You know you have the real gospel when God gets all the glory in it and through it.

When we live from the power of the gospel (Christ) for the purpose of the gospel (God's glory), our good and his glory become intertwined.

Our Good and God's Glory Linked as One Pursuit

Life is always going to be hard. The sooner we come to grips with this fact the sooner we can stop wasting our time fooling around with unhelpful solutions focused on making the world perfect. Jesus didn't say to move somewhere where the storms never come. He said you should build your house on the rock, on him, because storms always come in this life and only he can keep us stable (Matthew 7:24-27).

Everything is solved when God is our everything, when our joy is built on nothing but him. When he is the treasure we seek, we will always have the joy and motivation to do whatever is before us. We will never overcome difficulties and temptations by bearing down and trying harder. We will only overcome the pitfalls of this life when we realize, by his grace, the pleasure we seek in self-centered satisfactions can never compare to the soul quenching love of God. We will overcome the hardships of this life not by running and hiding like soldiers on the retreat, but by fighting back with a passionate, relentless pursuit of a greater pleasure in a greater God than this world could ever offer. We must love God's presence more than we fear pain if we are to survive on this planet.

Jesus wasn't willing to die such a brutal death because he was a masochist. Rather, he could leave heaven and endure earth because he was a holy hedonist, able to endure painful times because of his greater desire for pleasure in his Father, "For the joy set before him he endured the cross, scorning its shame, and sat down at the right hand of the throne of God. Consider him who endured such opposition from sinners, so that you will not grow weary and lose heart" (Hebrews 12:2-3).

We are to consider how Christ endured his cross so we will know how to carry ours. He bore our shame because he was motivated by the end goal of pleasure produced through being right next to his Father forever. We too have the power to endure whatever this life will throw at us because we know we have a greater reward in God for eternity compared to the sacrifices required of us now (2 Corinthians 2:16-18).

When his presence is our heart's desire, no problem is too great for us to handle because we know our faithful endurance will result in a greater, God-centered reward. So to close, I think it fitting to end with one last C.S. Lewis quote:

> The New Testament has lots to say about self-denial, but not about self-denial as an end in itself. We are told to deny ourselves and to take up our crosses in order that we may follow Christ; and nearly every description of what we shall ultimately find if we do so contains an appeal to desire. If there lurks in most modern minds the notion that to desire our own good and earnestly to hope for the enjoyment of it is a bad thing, I submit that this notion has crept in. . . and is no part of the Christian faith. Indeed, if we consider the unblushing promises of reward and the staggering nature of the rewards promised in the Gospels, it would seem that Our Lord finds our desires not too strong, but too weak. We are half-hearted creatures, fooling about with drink and sex and ambition when infinite joy is offered us, like an ignorant child who wants to go on making mud pies in a slum because he cannot imagine what is meant by an offer of a holiday at the sea. We are far too easily pleased.[6]

Our best life will be experienced when God's praise and our pleasure become the same pursuit. He is our greatest joy and our hearts will find no rest until they rest in him. May God grant us the grace to love him for his glory and our good as they truly are intertwined forever.

Works Cited

Chapter 1:

1. Lewis, C.S. *Mere Christianity.*
2. *Edwards, Jonathan.* Quote from John Piper's *God's Passion for His Glory*, p.92.

Chapter 2:

1. Lewis, C.S. *Mere Christianity.*
2. Tozer, A.W. *The Knowledge of the Holy* (New York: HarperCollins, 1978), 1.

Chapter 3:

1. Brother Lawrence. *The Practice of the Presence of God.* New Kenisington: Whitaker House, 1982. P.34.
2. Lewis, C.S. *Mere Christianity.*
3. St. Augustine.

Chapter 4:

1. Bonhoeffer, Dietrich. *The Cost of Discipleship.* New York: New York (1974), p.339.
2. Edwards, Jonathan (Quote taken from John Piper's *God's Passion for His Glory, p33.)*
3. Keller, Tim. Paraphrase from the sermon "The Search for Happiness" http://sermons2.redeemer.com/sermons/search-happiness.
4. Lewis, C.S. *God in the Dock.* Grand Rapids: Michigan (2014), p.309-310.

5. Lewis, C.S. *The Complete C.S. Lewis Signature Classics (Mere Christianity)*. New York: New York (2002), p.36.

Chapter 5:

1. Lewis, C.S. *The Problem of Pain* (New York: HarperCollins Publishers, 1996), pp. 46-47.
2. Lucado, Max. *It's Not About Me* (Brentwood, TN: Integrity Publisher, 2004), pp. 26.
3. Tozer, A.W. *The Pursuit of God.*
4. Piper, John. *God's Passion for His Glory*, p.41.
5. Lewis, C.S. *The Complete C.S. Lewis Signature Classics (The Problem of Pain)*. New York: New York (2002), p.576.
6. Lewis, C.S. *Mere Christianity.*

Chapter 6:

1. Spurgeon, Charles. From the sermon, "Bought with a Price."
   http://www.spurgeon.org/sermons/1004.htm
2. Lewis, C.S. *The Four Loves.*

Chapter 7:

1. Tozer, A.W. *The Root of the Righteous.*
2. Lewis, C.S. *God in the Dock.*

Chapter 8:

1. Lewis, C.S. *The Problem of Pain.*
2. Ibid.

Chapter 9:

1. http://www.history.army.mil/moh/vietnam-a-l.html#BENAVIDEZ
2. http://www.voiceforthedefenseonline.com/story/presidents-message-roy-benavidez-inspiring-american-hero%E2%80%94-reminder-defense-lawyer-have-faith-d
3. Chambers, Oswald *My Utmost for His Highest.* Grand Rapids: Discovery House Publishers, 1963. P.247.

Chapter 10:

1. MacDonald, George. *Unspoken Sermons.* Feather Trail Press, 2009. P.71.
2. MacArthur, John. *The Prodigal Son.* Nashville: Thomas Nelson, 2008. P. 127-129.
3. http://www.spurgeon.org/sermons/2073.htm
4. Stott, John. *Basic Christianity.* Inter-Varsity Press, 1971. P. 102.

Chapter 11:

1. Lewis, C.S. *The Four Loves.*

Chapter 12:

1. Lewis, C.S. *Mere Christianity.*
2. Chambers, Oswald. *My Utmost for His Highest.* Grand Rapids: Discovery House Publishers, 1963. P.50.
3. Lewis, C.S. *The Four Loves.*

Chapter 13:

1. Brother Lawrence. *The Practice of the Presence of God.* New Kenisington: Whitaker   House, 1982. P.32.
2. Piper, John. *Desiring God.* Colorado Springs: Multnomah Books, 2011. P. 10.
3. Lewis, C.S. *Mere Christianity.*
4. Piper, John. *God's Passion for His Glory.* p76
5. Piper, John. *Desiring God.* Colorado Springs: Multnomah Books, 2011. P. 25.
6. Lewis, C.S. *The Weight of Glory.* Grand Rapids: Eerdmans, 1965. P.1-2.

For blogs, free eBooks, and resources by Mark Ballenger, please visit ApplyGodsWord.com.

Contact us at:
Twitter: @Apply_GodsWord
Facebook: www.facebook.com/ApplyGodsWord/
Website: ApplyGodsWord.com
Email: markballenger@applygodsword.com

Printed in Great Britain
by Amazon

85774448R00105